Coaching Knock Your Socks Off Service

Be sure to take a look at the other books in AMACOM's best-selling KNOCK YOUR SOCKS OFF series!

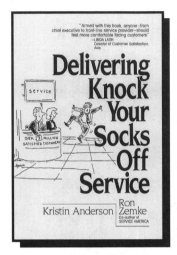

Paperback • $16.95

Paperback • $15.95

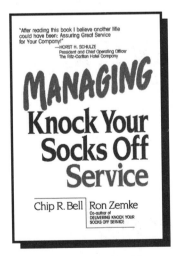

Paperback • $17.95

Paperback • $17.95

Available at your local bookstore, or call 1-800-262-9699.

Coaching Knock Your Socks Off Service

Ron Zemke & Kristin Anderson

Authors of the bestselling DELIVERING KNOCK YOUR SOCKS OFF SERVICE
and KNOCK YOUR SOCKS OFF ANSWERS

amacom

American Management Association

New York • Atlanta • Boston • Chicago • Kansas City • San Francisco • Washington, D.C.
Brussels • Mexico City • Tokyo • Toronto

Library of Congress Cataloging-in-Publication Data
Zemke, Ron.
    Coaching knock your socks off service / Ron Zemke & Kristin
Anderson.
        p.   cm.
    Includes bibliographical references.
    ISBN 0-8144-7935-9
    1. Customer services.   2. Supervision of employees.   3. Mentoring
in business.   4. Employee motivation.   5. Employees—Counseling of.
I. Anderson, Kristin.   II. Title.
HF5415.5.Z459   1996
658.3'14—dc20   96–34196
                                                           CIP

Printing number

20 19 18 17 16

Contents

Acknowledgments   *xi*

Introduction: The World of the Customer Service Coach   *xiii*

1 Thinking and Acting Like a Coach   **1**
- From Boss to Coach
- The Content of Coaching
- The Importance of Preparation
- Coach as Performance Problem Solver
- The Dreaded Reprimand

2 Skills of the Knock Your Socks Off Service Coach   **14**
- Gathering Data
  Cautions
- Providing Feedback
  Display Feedback
  Troubleshooting Your Display Feedback System
  Interpersonal Feedback
- Questioning
  Listening Helps
- Informing and Instructing
- Providing Positive Reinforcement
  Lasting Value

**3 "Welcome to the Team!" Coaching the
New Employee**   **33**
- Getting Off on the Right Foot
- The Disney Approach
- Step 1: Welcoming

- Step 2: Orientation
  Listening to the New Employee
  The Expectations Discussion
  The Agenda
- Step 3: Training
  Training in What?
  Where Training Comes From
- Step 4: Transitioning
  When Training Is On-the-Job
  When Formal Training Is Available
  Welcome Them Back—and Help Them Apply What
  They've Learned

4 **"Nice Job, Charlene!" Coaching for High
   Performance**   **48**
   - Situation 1: Charlene's Big Presentation
   - Situation 2: Then There's Charlie
- Spot Incentives
- Spotlight the Performance
- Caution
- Job Well Done

5 **"Can I Help?" Coaching on the Run**   **56**
   - Coaching on the Run . . . With Care
   Step 1: Observe First
   Step 2: Pick an Action
     - Situation 1: The Case of the Cranky Guest
     - Situation 2: The Case of the Confused Software Buyer
     - Situation 3: The Case of the Screaming Mimi

6 **"Help! I'm Stumped." Coaching the Unsure
   Employee**   **66**
   - Twenty Questions—Abbreviated
   - The Hot Hand-Off Follow-Up

7 **"This Could Be Tricky." Coaching for
   Difficult Duty**   **73**
   - Situation 1: The Case of the Tardy Title Search
   - Situation 2: The Case of the Icky Ice Cream

8 "Great Opportunity, Charlie!" Coaching for Special Situations   **84**
- What Constitutes a Growth Opportunity?
  - Situation 1: The Senior Management Presentation
  - Situation 2: The Case of the Assistant Coach

9 The Coach's Nasty Nine   **91**
- Dr. Tom's Sure-Fire Coaching Conference
  Step 1: Position the Discussion
  Step 2: The Discussion
  Step 3: Agree on a Course of Action
  Step 4: Set a Follow-Up Date
- Simple Performance Adjustments
  Getting the Rules Right: "What Do You Mean You Comp'ed Everyone's Meal?"
  - Situation 1: Charlie Gives Away the Store
  - Situation 2: The Case of the Disputed Shipping Charges
  Coaching From Customer Reports: "And the Survey Says . . . ."
  - Situation 1: "That Charlene, She Walks on Water!"
  - Situation 2: "You Oughta Fire That Charlene Bozo!"
  - Situation 3: "That Charlene Stinks. I'm Never Coming Back to This Stupid Restaurant Again. Signed, An Ex-Customer"
  - Situation 4: "You People Really Stink! I Waited Forty Minutes for a Table, and Then When I Got One, the Friday Fish Fry Special Was All Sold Out."
  - Situation 5: Coaching Around Hearsay—"Your Road Repair People Are a Bunch of Goof-Offs!"
  The Slumping Employee: "I'm Not Concerned About Tom's Output Right Now. What I Am Concerned About Is Your Performance."
  - Situation 1: The Sales Call Slide
  - Situation 2: The Never-Going-to-Make-It Employee
- Performance Adjustments in Complex Times
  The Employee Who Is Hard to Replace: "I Don't Want You to Get Mad and Quit, But . . . ."

- Situation 1: Low Unemployment
- Situation 2: Low Employee Commitment
- Situation 3: Scarcity of Skilled Labor
- Situation 4: Managing Diversity
- Situation 5: With Friends Like These . . .

The Employee You Don't Own, and Can't Fire: "You're Not the Boss Over Me."
- Situation 1: Dr. Bad Mouth
- Situation 2: The Officious Office Service

Troublesome Personal Habits: "What Do You Mean, I Stink?"
- Situation 1: Chatty Cathy
- Situation 2: Hugging Hank
- Situation 3: Smelly Sam
- Situation 4: Farting Freda
- Situation 5: Temperamental Ted
- Trouble on the Team

Reluctance to Change: "I Know You Hate the New Computer System."
- Situation 1: System Changes
- Situation 2: "What Happened to Charlene?"

Intramural Moaning: "I Don't Care if You Don't Like the Marketing Department or Jane. You Still Need to Work With Them."
- Situation 1: "Deal With It"
- Situation 2: When Accounting Says No

When You Aren't the Expert: "Hey, I'm the Computer Expert, So You Just Do Your Manager Stuff and Leave Me Alone to Do My Job."
- Situation 1: "Look, You Have to Be a Techno-Nerd to Really Understand This"
- Situation 2: "Look, You're New Around Here. You Don't Understand the Way We Do Things and Why We Do Them That Way."

10 "Can We Talk?" Peer Coaching   128
- The Supportive Environment
- Awareness of the Limits

- The Four-Step Peer Coaching Model
  Step 1: Positioning
  Step 2: Discussion
  Step 3: Advice Giving
  Step 4: Closure
- The Art of Accepting Peer Coaching
- The Peer Support Model in Action
  - Situation 1: The Contentious Encounter
  - Situation 2: The Venomous Voice
  - Situation 3: "You Tell That Clerk She's the Rudest Person I Ever Met!"
- Training for Positive Peer Coaching
- Variation: When the Peer Involved in Peer Support Is You

11 Recommended Resources   144
- Books
- Newsletters
- Other Resources

About the Authors   *147*

Acknowledgments

What's that old shibboleth? Oh, yes! Success has a thousand parents. Failure is an orphan. Well, this book is a success. And it has a pretty good bloodline, to boot.

The first in line for our thanks are Drs. Tom Connellan and Chip Bell, our constant partners in crime and writing, who you will see referenced throughout. Their mark is upon this book in a hundred ways. Another strong, strong influence on the content and style of this book—particularly the shape of many of the process tracks—is Susan Zemke, spouse of Ron Zemke, and a skilled and knowledgeable coach and trainer of coaches.

A second group of thankees are John Bush, Dave Zielinski, and Mary Glenn. The indelible mark of John Bush—artist, illustrator, wild mind—is everywhere, literally from cover to cover. And *on* both covers. Dave "Z-man" Zielinski's influence is more subtle, though no less obvious to us. Dave stitched our chapters together, brought us up short when our explanations and examples were bad or corny, and found all the places where we managed to contradict ourselves without knowing it. Editor Mary Glenn of AMACOM owns our souls. Without her encouragement and championing, there would be no book. Her tolerance for ambiguity—and missed deadlines—is truly amazing. And through it all, she absolutely believed we could do this in the ridiculous time frame we set for ourselves.

Last, but certainly not least, on our thank-you list are the service pros who trekked through the snow, rain, sleet, and cold of the winter of 1995–96 to focus group centers and meeting rooms across the country to teach us about the *real* challenges of coaching for customer service success.

To each and every one of you who contributed so mightily to this book, Thank you—*you* knocked *our* socks off!

Ron Zemke
Kristin Anderson
May 1996

Introduction

The World of the Customer Service Coach

"Coaching subordinates isn't an addition to a manager's job; it's an integral part of it."

—George S. Odiorne

The questioner was a very successful, award-winning life and casualty insurance general agent, well known in South Georgia as a good boss and a good developer of people. And his question at the seminar was an insightful, right-on-the-money probe.

> "I was walking through the office the other day and heard one of my people on the phone hassling with an old, long-time customer. When she hung up, I sat down and told her I'd heard the end of her conversation, and asked if I could help. We went through the whole scenario, and I talked her through how she might have asked a different question here or made a different suggestion there, and then we agreed on a follow-up to the customer's call."

> "Sounds to me as if you covered all the bases, Bill."

> "Oh, I know. That's not the question part. What I'm curious about is, how long am I going to have to be

coaching my person like this? When will I have her empowered?"

"How long has she been with you?"

"Oh, coming on eleven years."

Both the content and the context of Bill's tongue-in-cheek
bemusement struck a chord with us. Here was a very capable
manager, with a high-performing, loyal, effective employee. Yet
Bill was wondering whether one or the other of them—he or the
employee—wasn't in some way a failure. On the one hand, he
was asking whether *he* was a failure for not being able to make
the employee a freestanding, fully functioning, not in need of
overseeing individual. On the other hand, he was wondering
whether *she* was a lost cause for needing coaching after eleven
years in the trenches.

As we listened, it seemed to us that Bill was being led ever
so slightly astray by his desire to be the best manager possible.
It is our view that a fully functioning, empowered employee *is
not necessarily or desirably* an employee free of the need for feedback, counsel, and, occasionally, correction. And that Bill Smith
is far from a management failure.

By analogy, the best performers in the world of sport and
the performing arts never outgrow their need for coaching. Professional tennis players like Pete Sampras, Andre Agassi, or
Steffi Graf are watched over by hawk-eyed coaches, ever alert
for the appearance of unconscious bad habits and lapses of judg-
ment in their game. Seasoned golfers on the men's and women's
PGA tours routinely went in search of the late Harvey Penick,
coach of choice to golf's greats for decades, at the first sign of
developing an unintended hook or slice. And for every Tom
Hanks, Julia Roberts, or Emma Thompson who wins kudos and
awards for acting, there is a Ron Howard, Sidney Pollack, or
Steven Spielberg—a skilled director/coach—who is there every
step of the way, giving feedback and assistance.

This attention to detail, and the unabashed search for help
when their games have gone a bit awry, pays off handsomely for
the sporting and acting set. In 1995, for instance, the difference
in earnings between the number-one and number-fifty money

winners on the PGA tour was over a million dollars. But the shot production difference between the number-one and number-fifty money winners was less than one stroke per round played, averaged across the entire season, according to PGA statistics.

The difference between the top performers and the also-rans in every field is in the details, and those top performers depend emphatically on the coaching skills of the Harvey Penicks and Bill Smiths and Ron Howards of the world, who can, and gladly do, come to their aid when their games are off. Good coaching helps first-rate firing-line performers to be their best each and every time they face a tough tee, a tricky backhand, a tongue-twisting line, or an upset customer. And the need for good coaching, like the need for nutrition and rest, recognition and reward, is something the best players never outgrow. The truly empowered, self-directed customer service employee is one who, like the professional athlete, actor, or musician, knows when he or she needs the guiding hand of a top-notch coach. It is rarely the one who thinks he or she has nothing more to learn, no skill in need of improvement, no need to look for a better way.

Given the philosophy that frontline performers—or any of us, for that matter—"never outgrow the need for coaching," you would think that coaching would be a normal, natural, high-priority part of every manager's and supervisor's day. You'd think that, but according to several recent studies, you'd be wrong!

• A study of U.S. and European companies conducted by the Conference Board identified poor or insufficient job performance feedback (a critical part of coaching) as the number-one cause of individual employee performance problems in 60 percent of the companies surveyed.

• Development Dimensions International, a Pittsburgh-based consulting firm, surveyed 1,149 people at 79 companies and found managers' feedback and coaching skills to be sorely lacking. Overall satisfaction with coaching and feedback was rated 3.5 on a scale of 1 to 5 by employees and managers alike. And the effectiveness of the performance appraisal process was given a rollicking 2.9 on the same scale. Hardly a ringing endorsement.

- A 1994 study of salespeople conducted by the University of Missouri found that out of a wide range of skills, managers were rated lowest on their ability to give employees useful feedback on job performance.

Okay. Given these bleak research findings, perhaps our premise is wrong. Perhaps coaching is important only for athletes, actors, dancers, and singers—not for salespeople, customer service reps, and accountants. After all, you and we know a lot of successful businesspeople who can't turn back flips, score touchdowns, recite Shakespeare, play the flute, carry a tune, or turn a pirouette. It's possible. Possible, but not likely.

And certainly not according to Dr. Lois P. Frankel and Dr. Karen L. Otazo.* When Frankel and Otazo asked frontline employees about the characteristics of managers who motivated them to do their best work, they learned that there are ten traits these memorable managers had in common:

- Took time to listen to me.
- Saw me as a person, not just an employee.
- Cared about my personal problems.
- Set a positive example.
- Let me know I was capable of more.
- Encouraged me.
- Never pulled rank—often pitched in.
- Let me know what was going on.
- Praised me for a job well done.
- Was straightforward when I didn't do a job well.

Those behaviors—listening, setting a positive example, giving praise, pointing out improvement areas, and encouraging employees to stretch and grow—are very much the skills of the Knock Your Socks Off Service coach. All of which leads us to a puzzling and important question.

*Lois P. Frankel and Karen L. Otazo, "Employee Coaching: The Way to Gain Commitment, Not Just Compliance," *Employment Relations Today* (Autumn 1992, pp. 311–320).

Why Then Are Managers Such Poor Coaches?

Most managers are weak coaches, and most employees know it. As do the managers themselves. Why so? To find out, we have been asking employees and managers in seminars and focus groups to tell us why, if good coaching is so important, good coaching is so rare. According to these employees and managers, there are at least four reasons.

• *Confrontation reluctance.* No one likes confrontation. And coaching can seem like an open invitation to wrangling and hard feelings. Managers preparing to discuss performance with even a highly competent employee conjure up scenes of dread in their minds. "I tell an employee that there is room for improvement, and then what happens? Tears. Recriminations. Accusations. No, thank you! I'd rather skip the whole thing. This playing God, it's not for me." Reluctance is an especially important factor when the manager isn't as expert as the employee. "I know I should be in there helping, but I don't know this software half as well as some of the reps. How can I coach that?" one supervisor confided.

• *Fear of offending.* No one really likes to upset other people. Sometimes just the offer of coaching can be interpreted as a criticism of an employee's performance. "Look, some of these people have been on the phones here seven, eight seasons. I start trying to give them advice—and look out. They take it very personally. Like I was saying they were bad people or something," observed the new manager of a mail-order call center.

• *Fear of failure.* Coaching is a learnable skill, but one that most managers have never mastered. And they know it. "I know I should do it. But, hey, I'm not Knute Rockne. I get embarrassed and flustered trying to give pep talks," is the attitude! Employees routinely report that managers are better at pointing out job performance problems than at helping employees work through them. As one frustrated customer service employee we interviewed put it, "Most of the time I know when I'm screwing up. Where I need the help is getting out of trouble, not knowing I'm in it!"

- *No time for coaching.* As businesses continue to downsize, consolidate, and ask people to do more and more, the time available for any task goes down. We frequently hear: "I'd love to be able to work with my people. But I'm on the line, too. There isn't any time for coaching anybody anymore."

But coaching needn't be feared or offend. And it is certainly learnable. And done well, it gives time, it doesn't take time away from other tasks. And you don't need to be Lou Holtz, Vince Lombardi, or Knute Rockne to be a good coach for your employees. You don't even have to *know* who Lou Holtz, Vince Lombardi, and Knute Rockne *are* to be a successful coach.* Coaching is a process that, in fact, begins long before an employee has a performance problem, or needs help with a tough customer, or has developed a single bad habit. Coaching, done properly, is a positive, skill-building, confidence-affirming process that is only occasionally—and sparingly—about correction. Most of the time, coaching is about adding polish to already skillful performance, about increasing employees' problem-fixing options and repertoire, and about helping good employees take on new challenges.

Over the last two years, we—like Frankel and Otazo—have queried customer service managers and employees about successful on-the-job coaches and coaching that have helped them perform better, work more effectively, and feel positive about themselves, their customers, their coworkers, and the work itself. This book is the end result of our quest to define the ideas and actions master managers bring to the task of creating and delivering Knock Your Socks Off Coaching.

About This Book

There are eleven short chapters in this short book. The first two, "Thinking and Acting Like a Coach" and "Skills of the Knock Your Socks Off Service Coach," address the basic philosophy

---

*Factoid: All three are legendary football coaches well known for their macho histrionics, which brings up another semi-important point: You don't have to have played sports or even like sports to be a good coach.

and skills of effective coaching. Chapters 3 through 10 address the most common—and critical—coaching situations.

- *"Welcome to the Team!" Coaching the New Employee.* Orienting and training new employees is a key coaching opportunity. An employee is never more open to learning than during the first few days on the job. The best coaches use that focus and motivation to enfold the new employee in the organization's vision and communicate its core values, not just to set the employee off on the right path to the lunchroom.
- *"Nice Job, Charlene!" Coaching for High Performance.* Giving praise is an important, undervalued, and underdone coaching "must." There are multiple ways of ensuring that frontline service pros know that they are valued and how they are doing, and for ensuring that praise comes across as authentic, not hollow. Positive feedback, recognition, and reward are the breakfast food of both service superstars and star athletes.
- *"Can I Help?" Coaching on the Run.* Good coaches, like Bill Smith, frequently have opportunities to do on-the-spot coaching without much prep time. We look at a sure-fire structure for the on-the-spot performance discussion, as well as a list of do's and don'ts that makes the difference between helping and creating resentment.
- *"Help! I'm Stumped." Coaching the Unsure Employee.* Every coach has had an employee come asking for help. The way that help is delivered makes the difference between employee dependence and employee empowerment, between employees who are confident in themselves and those who seem perpetually needy.
- *"This Could Be Tricky." Coaching for Difficult Duty.* Some customer service tasks are darned hard and more than a little tricky. Preparing an employee for the difficult ones creates confidence, and ensures that tough customers remain repeat customers.
- *"Great Opportunity, Charlie!" Coaching for Special Situations.* Nothing motivates some people like a new chance to shine in the eyes of others by tackling a "stretch" task. With a little help from a great coach, they eagerly come back for more.

- *The Coach's Nasty Nine.* In this chapter, we look at the real coaching situations that managers and supervisors like yourself say they have had the toughest time responding to—what we call the "nasty nine."

- *"Can We Talk?" Peer Coaching.* More and more companies are moving to self-managed or leaderless groups. Great, but that doesn't negate the need for coaching. It just changes the name on the clipboard. Peer coaching need not be an oxymoron like military intelligence or airline food, or necessarily a frightening endeavor, as long as the ground rules are clear.

A Word About Words . . . and an Assignment

Rather than make up a random sampling of strange names, we have invented two "everyperson" customer service reps who seem always to be in need of coaching and counseling: Charlie and Charlene. So to every reader named Charlie and Charlene—nothing personal. Also, be advised that we have willy-nilly alternated "he" and "she," and "him" and "her," "his" and "hers," and, of course, "Charlie" and "Charlene." We have no idea how sexually balanced our pronouning has been. We had a few better things to do than corral and count our pronouns by gender.

And now for the assignment. We have proposed solutions to forty or so coaching situations. You may not—probably will not—agree with all of our solutions. Fine. But don't just wrinkle your nose and stick out your tongue, or shake your head and turn the page when you find yourself in disagreement with one of our solutions. Instead, stop, take pen and pad, and write out your *own* solution. When you're done, put it in the book—in the back, in the front, maybe right where the offending solution is. But keep it someplace where you can retrieve it when next you encounter that situation. If you care enough to send a copy to us as well, that would be okay.

So, with all that taken care of, it's time to get on with it. Good reading and good luck, Coach. The game is Monday, and you've got your work cut out for you.

> ``It is important to understand that there are no topics or problems that a manager should not discuss with an employee *if they affect the employee's work*.''
>
> —Dennis C. Kinlaw

Coaching Knock Your Socks Off Service

1

Thinking and Acting Like a Coach

"It is easy to get the players. Gettin' 'em to play together, that's the hardest part."

—Casey Stengel

Chances are pretty good that you didn't become a manager or supervisor by accident. You didn't just stumble into work one day and find a title change on your time card, someone new sitting at your old desk, and your personal possessions moved to a new office with your name, followed by the word "manager," on the door.

More than likely, you aimed and angled, trained and studied, made your aspirations well known, and spent time quizzing everyone within friendly earshot about what it would take to make the leap to the managerial ranks. And chances are that from time to time, your boss asked you to fill in, gave you opportunities to manage projects, put you in front of his or her boss to show your mettle, and generally mentored you along the road from worker bee to manager. You aspired, you worked, and you attained your goal.

And one of the first things you learned when you became a manager, after everyone had shaken your hand and wished you well, was that nobody is crazy about bosses—even if the boss is good old lovable you! That probably came as a surprise, although it shouldn't have. The concept of "boss" takes shape for most of us long before we enter the workforce. Encounters, good and bad, with authority figures—parents and teachers, ministers

1

and scoutmasters, professors and drill instructors—shade and shape the way we think and feel about bosses, and being bossed about. To most employees, *boss* is a four-letter word.

From Boss to Coach

Fortunately, there isn't much enthusiasm today for "bossing" in the world of work. Most organizations are enlightened to the point where they actively encourage managers to lead, rather than to boss. To ask, rather than to tell. To influence, rather than to intimidate. To encourage and support, rather than threaten or bully.

The purpose of coaching is to help an individual customer service representative improve in a specific area of his or her job or enhance or extend a valuable skill in a new way.

It is particularly vital in service-sensitive organizations, divisions, and departments that managers see themselves as leaders and coaches—not as bosses. It is more consistent with the nature of the service process and positive service outcomes than the old "bull-in-the-woods boss" model of managing.

Directing the performance of a service, as opposed to supervising the production of a product, means that you are very dependent on your employees—not machines or computerized processes—to create positive customer outcomes and experiences. In the world of service delivery, your people are your prime production asset. It is their direct, personal, put-themselves-on-the-line, face-to-face, real-time interactions with customers that you are there to support and keep focused and sharp. Customer service is the kind of hot, personal, intimate activity that product creation and delivery can never be.

Because of the very personal nature of customer service, the way you manage customer service employees has some unique attributes. You are a closely scrutinized role model, and employees take their service cues directly from you. The way you treat (or just talk about) customers in view and earshot of your people has a profound effect on how they perform, how they view their jobs and the organization, and the effort they'll put forward to serve customers.

Remember the old canard, "Do what I say, not what I do"? As leader of a customer service team, what you say, what you do, and the way you say it and do it strongly influence what your people do on the job with their customers. To your employees, your behavior and demeanor are a reflection of the real rules of the organization.

At the same time, once you step into the role of manager/ leader, you are no longer an active player with *direct* influence on customers. You can—and should—be a role model of good service through the way you deal with peers, colleagues, employees, and the occasional customer. You can and must support your employees' efforts. But in the last analysis, once you have left the line to manage, even if you fill in from time to time, you become dependent on your employees, not the other way around.

In the last analysis, they make the customers happy—or horrified. They fix the problems—or don't. They cool the overheated and mollify the miffed—not you. You may diagram the plays, write the scripts, and direct the action, but as manager, leader, and coach, you will never again be seen as a player.

The Content of Coaching

There are some striking similarities between your responsibilities as a service coach and the responsibilities of coaches in athletics and the arts:

You instill fundamentals. Your people have to know how to play their particular roles or positions. What to do, and when and how to do it. What to say, and why. They need to know where they should be when the customer feeds them a cue or throws them a curve. And just as great actors and athletes know the necessity of constant practice, of "getting in the reps" (repetitions) that help them master the part they are called on to play, you have to help your people stay focused on the task and constantly hone their skills.

You build teamwork. The second baseman is one of nine players on the baseball field. The violinist sitting in the first chair is just one player in the orchestra. No matter how individually talented he or she may be, the overall success of the production—be it a baseball game or a Beethoven symphony—is judged by how well everyone plays together. You position your players. You have to make sure they know how their roles interlock with those of others on the service team. You have to keep them focused on both their individual performance and the overall success of the group. You keep the group working together in harmony.

You evaluate and adjust. Every team starts with a game plan. But the plan can only prepare; it can't control play from start to finish. There are other variables, often not subject to anyone's control, that have to be taken into account in the midst of the performance. Like a sports coach, a service manager has to know how to reposition players, change the strategy, react to immediate needs, and anticipate circumstances that may be encountered in the next quarter or the next act.

You reinforce and motivate. The coach's role is to correct problems without destroying a player's self-confidence, and to praise good efforts without giving the recipient of the "well done's" a swelled head. You can't play favorites and build a united team.

You can't preach sacrifice and dedication and then go put your feet up while your people give everything they've got. Your words and actions set the tone for theirs.

The Importance of Preparation

Before they take the field or the stage, players have to have a good idea of what they're going to be doing and how their individual performances will combine into a cohesive group effort.

In sports, preparation involves knowing specific actions to take in specific circumstances—with a player on first, the shortstop throws to second base on a ground ball to get the double play; when there's no one on, the play is at first base.

In the arts, there's a script or musical score to learn, often augmented by "marks" to hit when delivering a line or a conductor's modifications in tempo and volume that provide subtle changes in the look and sound of the performance.

First-rate service organizations prepare their players in similar ways. At Disneyland and Walt Disney World, for example, the men and women who make the rides and attractions "go" work from carefully planned and memorized scripts, complete with exceptions, situational variations, and approved modifications—ad libs, in other words. They know where they're supposed to be and what they're supposed to do, including how to take charge of a potentially negative situation and turn it into a positive for their guests. Disney's service deliverers practice a performance art. And they are performers every bit as much as an actor, actress, or athlete, and their managers every bit as much coaches.

Coach as Performance Problem Solver

Every coach is faced with the puzzle of how to bring his or her team to a peak performance level and keep it there. To accomplish that, the Knock Your Socks Off Service coach must be flexible in his or her approach, as flexible as he or she expects the frontline service employee to be in meeting a customer's unique, special, idiosyncratic needs, wants, and expectations. Nowhere is that more important than in the service coach's efforts to help individual performers reach and sustain high levels of performance. The seasoned service coach, while flexible, has a preplanned performance management approach for every situation.

When the employee is performing well. Tailored, targeted recognition, reward, and feedback are often the key. The adage "different strokes for different folks" is very apt. When performance is superior and the performer is appropriately challenged, the good coach searches for rewards valued by the individual. Does the star employee value taking on challenging cases? Helping to train new people? Gold stars on the wall? A chance to develop special skills? The Knock Your Socks Off Service coach knows what appeals and makes it available.

When the employee performs unevenly. Every coach has players whose performance is great some of the time, average at other times, and occasionally unacceptable. The astute coach praises the great outcomes and right behaviors, and encourages improvement in the subpar. Sometimes the coach provides helpful hints for improving the below-average performance—but the astute coach never delivers both praise *and* correction at the same time. When up-and-down performers hear, "Charlie, you're doing great on *this*, but you can do better on *that*," they don't hear the "doing great," they just hear the "do better" part. Sometimes, in fact, they can interpret your compliments as a not-so-subtle bribe to seduce improvement—"I really want you to buckle down *here*, so I'll throw you a pointless compliment over *there* to disarm your resistance"—in which case, you risk losing the power of the reward as well as distracting from the focus on improvement. Separate the "reward" part from the "encourage" part, and you help your people glow and grow.

When the employee hits a slump. Even the most seasoned, savvy performer can have a bad streak. Sometimes employees hit a slump or a lull during which everything seems to go wrong. Good coaches patiently communicate faith in the performer, especially when the results have been off and pride, confidence, and self-esteem are at their shakiest. They focus on and reinforce "the fundamentals," the good efforts that will eventually pay off: "That's the way to go, Charlene. Keep that up and I'm sure your sales (or service ratings, or renewal rates) will improve."

Two factors are at play in this approach. First, reinforcing the *process*—the behaviors known to lead to positive customer service results—keeps the employee focused on the right things, and decreases his or her temptation to start randomly making changes in hopes of improving results. Second, showing faith in the employee keeps his or her effort up and panic down.

Much has been written about the powerful influence a coach's expectations have on performance. It seems clear that demonstrating your belief in people often translates into performance improvement. It's a well-documented phenomenon that's sometimes referred to as the Pygmalion effect: If you think people will succeed (because you've put them in a position to do just that) and you treat them as if they will succeed, you're generally not going to be disappointed. The reverse is equally true: Expect the worse and you have a very good chance of getting it.

When the employee tries, fails, and can't figure out why—but you have a pretty good idea of what's going wrong. In this situation, most coaches will take the employee aside for a discussion. Our colleague Dr. Chip Bell calls these "advice-giving" sessions and suggests four guidelines for making the most of the discussion:

1. *Get agreement on the performance problem.*

   Coach: "Charlene, your call rate is below goal."

   Employee: "I know. And I've been trying to get my call length down, but it's not easy."

2. *Ask permission to give advice.*
   Advice is more easily accepted when the employee agrees to hear it.

   Coach: "As you know, I was monitoring calls this week, and I think I have some ideas. Are you up for hearing them?"

   Employee: "What do you have in mind?"

3. *Give the advice in the first person singular.*

> *Coach:*   "I noticed that some of your callers were real chatty. If it were me, I think I might try using a little creative silence. For instance, . . ."

4. *Get feedback on the usefulness of the advice.*

> *Coach:*   "We've talked about several ways to attack the call length problem. Do you think one of them might help?"

Advice-giving sessions work best when you are careful to avoid causing defensiveness and rejection of the advice. You accomplish that by proceeding slowly and with permission, involving the employee in the problem solving, avoiding judgmental language, and positioning yourself as helpful, friendly, and knowledgeable, not autocratic or "bossy."

A *variation* on the advice-giving session that some managers like is to make the discussion slightly more didactic through the use of questions and active listening. The key here is to ask genuine questions, not the accusing, empty, or leading sort. This is a useful variation when you know that the problem exists, but you don't know what the employee has been doing to rectify it. You want to avoid covering already well-plowed ground. For example:

> "Charlene, I know you've been working to get your call length down. Can you review what you've tried so far?"

or

> "Charlene, I know you were going to try several things to increase your average sales ticket. Can you tell me what's worked and what hasn't?"

or

"Charlene, would you bring me up to speed on what you've been doing to get more interviews?"

The performance coach should be seen as a mentor ("wise and trusted advisor"), not as an interrogator or a commander giving precise orders. Your goal is to assist and support in a manner that allows your help to be heard and accepted, but that leaves the accountability for improvement with the employee.

When the employee tries and fails, and neither the coach nor the employee has a clear idea why. This situation calls for careful analysis. More often than not, situations like this one have a wider impact than just on the single employee with the confounding problem. A careful assessment of what the employee is doing, and what the surrounding conditions are, sometimes shows a systemic problem that affects several areas of performance. For instance, Charlie tells you he is having a terrible time meeting his after-the-sale survey volume. Careful investigation suggests that the customer follow-up survey has been modified by marketing, and it is virtually impossible for a rep to meet the *old* goal for the number of follow-up calls per hour, using the questions on the *new* survey. The problem isn't *Charlie,* but a change in the task he and his peers are trying to accomplish.

There are at least *seven factors* you as the service coach should have in mind when looking for the *cause* of a rep's—or team's—performance shortfall:

1. *Task clarity.* Perhaps the performer is not clear on the performance you require. Would you bet your next year's salary that *your* view of the employee's accountabilities and expectations matches the *employee's* view of those key parameters? Asking, "Tell me what you are trying to accomplish in this situation" can lead to surprising insights.

2. *Task priority.* Sometimes failure is due to the performer's perception that the performance you expect is not really all that important. Does the employee's view of what's important match yours? Are there conflicting priorities?

"Charlene, there are a lot of demands in your job. Tell me how you see the importance of your various duties."

Are you, for instance, inadvertently demanding quality without explaining how to meet both quality and quantity goals? Or when and how to make the trade-off between the two?

3. *Competence.* Failure can sometimes be due to a simple lack of skill. People can't do well if they don't know how. Learning psychologist Robert Mager offers an easy test to determine whether you're facing a skill problem or a motivation issue: "Could he do the job if his life depended on it? If no, you have a training problem. If yes, you may have a performance gap that no amount of training can affect." Sitting next to or riding along with the employee, watching and listening, can give you insight into competence. So can simply asking something like, "Charlie, can you show me how you go about cutting off an overly long-winded customer?" and doing a little role-play.

4. *Obstacles.* Real or imagined physical and procedural barriers can interfere with good performance. Being told by a fellow employee, "Don't spend more than seventy seconds on a call. Long phone calls are the easiest way to get fired around here," makes that rule real in the employee's eyes, whether it is in fact real or simply hearsay. To the extent that you, as the coach, can modify or remove such barriers, you can free your people to perform better.

5. *Reward for failure.* Sometimes there's more reward for poor performance than for good performance. People who get attention (however negative) when they do poorly and are ignored when they do well may stop doing well just to get a reaction. You need to emphasize and comment on good performance and ignore small instances of poor performance when possible. Rule of thumb: Give three bits of positive recognition for every

negative or corrective comment, and you will be on the way to giving enough positives.

6. *Performance feedback.* Do you provide clear, timely information that helps your people evaluate and fine-tune their performance? Is this information useful and presented from a consistent perspective? Is it objective, verifiable, and clear? Or is it pointlessly general, only oral, and subject to weather-vane swings in emphasis that can confuse and disorient?

7. *Role–person mismatch.* When all else fails, you may need to reexamine whether the performer would be more successful in a different role or on a different team. Sometimes players who look good in tryouts or in the gym look less skillful on the field of play or on the stage in front of an audience. A customer service rep who can handle any single problem with great aplomb, but who folds under the pressure of ringing phones and thirty calls an hour, may be unsuited for the pace. But take care: Jumping directly to the "can't cut it" assessment can be a mistake. If the employee has been away from the firing line for a while, or is new to the pace of a live workload, his or her performance can quickly improve—with a little encouragement and help from you. Waiting and watching are critical to making the correct determination and setting the right course of action.

When the employee doesn't try, or seems to be actually trying to fail. This, in our experience, is a relatively rare situation—and one that is often hard to separate from the more common situations we've just described. Tread lightly before coming to the conclusion that the employee is being "willful" or acting in a "stubborn" or "malicious" way. Better for you to assume, as we do, that most employees want to do a good job, earn their pay, and avoid conflict with you, the organization, and their fellow employees. More often than not, these employees will welcome your coaching efforts and come back for more, once you have established yourself as a helpful, sympathetic, and respectful performance coach.

The Dreaded Reprimand

Sometimes, despite your best efforts at coaching and correcting, an employee will continue to behave in a way that is detrimental to customer satisfaction, team relations, and harmony, or even dangerous to him- or herself and others. It is very tempting at this point to start playing psychologist and spend time spinning scenarios in your head about the employee's dysfunctional ways and what you can do to intervene in the employee's collision course with unemployment.

Our advice—DON'T!

As human beings, we all want to reach out and help people who are in trouble. But the distraction of trying to "fix" one determinedly chronic problem employee can cause the performance of the team to suffer. Worse yet, you can inadvertently teach your team that performing poorly is the surest way to earn paid time away from the job. A manager who spends a lot of time trying to understand the psychology of the occasional problem employee, or who feels the need to involve him- or herself in employees' lives and learn "what makes them tick," runs the risk of crossing the line between the legitimate concerns of the business and unwarranted intrusion into employees' private lives. Management isn't about psychology, save in very minor, trivial ways. Management is about results and behavior. If you are getting the results you have asked people to produce, thank them and help them keep doing whatever it is that is working. If you're not getting the results, you—and they—have to figure out how to change what they are doing to get the results agreed upon. End of story.

Reprimands are designed to stop negative performance, but in such a way that performance can be improved without undermining self-esteem or leaving scar tissue. As Ken Blanchard, co-author of the *One-Minute Manager* books, is fond of saying, reprimanded performers should respond by focusing on what they need to do to improve, not on how they were treated by the person delivering the bad news. Most experts on employee discipline tell us that reprimands:

- Should be delivered in private.
- Should focus on performance rather than the person.
- Should be given with frankness, but not in anger.
- Should be appropriate to the infraction.

Good coaches do all of that, and one more thing: They underscore the impact that an individual's performance has on the team's performance. They know that it is far better to inspire people to avoid letting down their teammates or letting themselves down than to make them sweat to impress their coach. Performing well to impress the coach is the wrong goal!

The game of human achievement is played with complex game plans, changing rules, and ambiguous measurements. The coaches we admire on the sidelines at Saturday's game or behind the performance of a talented actor, musician, or dancer have much to teach us that's relevant for Monday's customer service challenge. At the same time, it is important not to overdo the sports and arts analogies. It isn't necessary to have ever coached an athletic team, or even played a sport or been a performing artist, to be a great Knock Your Socks Off Service coach. What is important is that you care enough to coach, and coach enough to affect your people in positive, affirming ways.

> ''The most personal strategy for building
> competence—and, therefore, one of the most
> powerful—is coaching. It is the one sure way in which
> managers can find out exactly what their employees
> do not know and what they need to know.''
>
> —Dennis C. Kinlaw

2

Skills of the Knock Your Socks Off Service Coach

''Good management consists of showing average people how to do the work of superior people.''

—John D. Rockefeller

Listen to the speechifying of a few successful sports coaches, and you can come away with the impression that ''recruitin' the best, workin 'em hard, inspirin' 'em to fight like heck, and showin' 'em you care'' is the key to creating a successful team. There are plenty of sports team coaches—and service managers as well—who swear that this is *indeed* the success formula to follow.

Watching successful coaches, however, tells a different story. Psychologist Thomas F. Gilbert did just that when he was a professor at the University of Alabama and Paul ''Bear'' Bryant was that institution's highly successful football coach. What did Gilbert discover? He found that Bryant did very little lecturing, inspiring, or even hugging and hollering at his players. What he did a lot of was watching—observing his players' movements in great detail. During practice, Bryant had videotape cameras stationed to capture the idiosyncrasies of his players' performance, and he kept meticulous performance charts for every player in every game. He gathered data. And when he saw a player consistently making an error—say a right tackle consistently had his feet out of position or a shoulder dropped the

wrong way—he told him about it, walked him through the proper procedure, watched him do it right, and—yes—gave him a "well done" for mastery when he had done it the right way. In Gilbert's words:

> "Bryant and his coaches treated the players almost exactly as if they were adult human beings. They told the boys where they stood, how much they were improving and what they could do to improve further. And they left it at that. All the hugging and hollering was saved until after a victory."*

Guess what? After observing and working with hundreds of first-rate Knock Your Socks Off Service managers, we've found that, like "Bear" Bryant, they too bring out the best in their teams through careful observation, information gathering, feedback, patient dialogue, and instruction—and some positive reinforcement when things go well.

*Thomas F. Gilbert and Marilyn B. Gilbert, "The Science of Winning," *Training* magazine (August 1988, pp. 33–40).

The Knock Your Socks Off Service coach's kit bag, then, is a simple but effective box containing five flexible and highly usable tools:

- Gathering data
- Providing feedback
- Questioning
- Informing and instructing
- Providing positive reinforcement

Gathering Data

The Knock Your Socks Off Service coach uses many kinds of data to keep his or her unit on track and his or her people aware of their performance and focused on progress. Key among the kinds of data the effective coach uses are:

- *Performance data.* Performance data are generally about outcomes: calls handled per unit time, customers interviewed, sales made, dollars per sale, orders taken—any outcome that is the result of the customer service person's efforts. Performance data are generally anything that can be easily measured in a yes or no fashion. Yes, the lab technician did the test, or no, it didn't take place. Yes, the software engineer solved the customer's problem, or no, he or she did not. If it can be graphed or charted, and seeing the graph or chart gives you or members of your team useful information, then it is probably performance data.
- *Customer satisfaction data.* Satisfaction data can come from customer surveys, focus groups, and customer panels. Satisfaction data can be quantitative, like the CS scores on a survey, or qualitative, like opinion and impression information gathered in focus groups. Quantitative satisfaction data can be charted and graphed just like performance data. Qualitative satisfaction data can be summarized in prose reports.
- *Customer contact data.* Letters and phone calls from happy or not-so-enthralled customers, and face-to-face conversations with the same folk, provide valuable "incident" information that can be used for individual or team coaching. *Mystery shop-*

ping, where a firm is hired to play-act the role of customer and evaluate your service, is the most highly organized form of customer contact data.

- *Personal observation data.* Working next to or riding along with a team member as he or she deals with "live" customers can be valuable. So can monitoring phone calls (a highly structured activity when done correctly). And so can simply sitting back and unobtrusively watching employees work with customers.

Cautions

There are some commonsense guidelines for the data gathering part of coaching:

- *Separate gathering and using data.* You can't do both at once. When you are gathering data, do that and only that. For instance, don't attempt to give an employee corrective feedback after watching one customer transaction. A single data point, whether it is an observed transaction or a dot on a production chart, is not enough information for taking any sort of meaningful action.

There are two exceptions to this rule: (1) When issues of safety or the law are involved, it is certainly appropriate to intercept a transaction you are observing, and set things straight. (2) When an employee is losing control of the transaction or himself, or a customer appears to be losing control, it is appropriate to step in (see Chapter 5, "Coaching on the Run").

- *Multiple data sources are best.* Basing a decision, or even a coaching discussion, on one *form* of data can be hazardous to performance improvement. Let's say you have discouraging sales or call-handling data on Charlie. His performance has been substandard for a week. You can certainly go to Charlie, mention what you've noticed, and ask, "Is there anything I can do to help you get your (call/sales) rate back up to par?" But until you gather more information, there isn't much you can do in a definitive way. The best use of data that suggest a performance problem is to *investigate further,* to gather more well-founded info.

• *Not all data are equal.* Do not overreact to a single customer complaint, or even a satisfaction survey that says that, on the average, customers aren't thrilled with your company. It is especially important that you *verify bad news* before you take any action. A complaint about Charlie pops up? Okay, ask him what he thinks led to the complaint. If you don't like Charlie's answer, watch Charlie's work for a while. Listen in on customer calls. Make up your own mind. Never take a single report or a nebulous interaction with a customer as a mandate to put Charlie in the stockade—use it as a signal to look further into Charlie's performance.

• *A single data point is* not *information.* Whether it's a dot on a performance chart, a customer letter, or a phone call from your boss, a single data point is just that: a single data point. On a graph, it takes three points to draft a trend. With *subjective* or *qualitative* data—focus groups, random calls, and so forth—you must be very careful not to overvalue (or undervalue) what you hear.

Data Give You Something to Think About—They Don't Tell You What to Think.

Providing Feedback

Feedback is information. It is information your customer service reps can use to *confirm* or *correct* their performance. Not just data, but specific information—knowledge—about their performance that tells them that they are performing "A-Okay," or that improvement is possible. *Feedback may be your most important coaching tool.*

For feedback to be of use, it must inform, enlighten, and clearly suggest what, if any, improvement is needed. Tell hotel housekeeping that "63.7 percent of the guests think their rooms are unacceptably messy after cleaning," and all that's been communicated is a generic "try harder and do better." The housekeepers know that there's a problem, but they have little idea of

what to do better. Instead, tell them, "Yesterday, 63.7 percent of the guests thought their rooms were unacceptably messy after cleaning" and that "wastebaskets weren't emptied on floors 5 through 11, used towels weren't replaced in rooms 410 through 421, and complaints about missing bath soap came from the fourth floor." Now the steps to correct the problem are clearer.

A word of caution about numbers and feedback: Percentages, averages, and proportions can make small numbers of problems seem like small potatoes as a result of "the law of unreported angst." Yet even small deviations from customer expectations can have a substantial impact on customer satisfaction and retention. In the hotel, for example, the guests in rooms 410 through 421 complaining about towels may seem like small potatoes. They are not. To the people in those eleven rooms, the towels are a very large problem. John Goodman of Technical Assistance Research Programs (TARP) reports that less than half of all unhappy customers complain. So if your department is averaging seventeen formal complaints a week, assume that there are *at least* seventeen *more* unhappy customers out there.

There are a number of ways to deliver feedback to your team. The two most useful ways of delivering feedback are via *display* and *interpersonally*, or through face-to-face *discussion*. Each communicates a different kind of information, and serves a different purpose.

Display Feedback

Display feedback is group or individual *performance data*—the tangible, visible, countable stuff—collected and displayed in a graph or chart for the team or individual to see and discuss. What gets charted? Practically anything can be charted and graphed. We know a professor of psychology who counted and charted personal thoughts to help him better focus his productive time. Many professional writers chart *writing time* and *pages produced.*

The best count and chart *pinpoints* or *targets* in the customer service environment are *outcomes.* Things like calls handled per hour or day or week. Transactions, shipments, deliveries made, customers contacted, problems solved.

Display feedback can become highly addictive. We all, it seems, love to know how we did today compared with yesterday, last week compared with this week, in our department compared with their department, in our company compared with the competition—and on it goes. Some organizations, like Federal Express, gather information on hundreds of service targets *a day.*

The best charts and graphs for customer service are the kind a human being can decipher (and make sense of) at a glance. This means that the display has to be large and uncluttered; the units of measure easily understood; the norms or standards of comparison clearly visible and easy to compare to actual performance. The chart in Figure 2-1 provides a good model of an effective display feedback chart.

This chart of inbound calls per hour shows at a glance:

- Current team performance
- The standard (15)
- The lower acceptable limit (10)
- The upper limit (20)*

*In many shops, coaches and their teams now set an "upper acceptable limit" for calls under the belief that quality suffers where the actual call rate is too high.

Figure 2-1. Team performance: customer service reps.

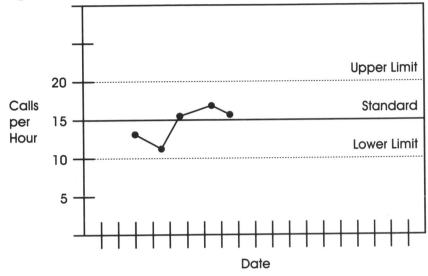

Dr. Thomas K. Connellan, a partner of ours, is one of North America's leading authorities on the use of feedback, recognition, and reward systems in maintaining high levels of quality service. He believes the best display feedback systems follow six principles:

1. *Display feedback works best when given in relation to a specific service quality goal.* Goal-directed behavior is very powerful behavior. Tell a new waiter or waitress that he or she waited on twenty customers tonight, and the first question you'll hear: "Is that good?" Useful feedback tells employees not only how they are doing, but how they are doing relative to the goals and performance standards they are expected to meet.

2. *Wherever possible, a display feedback system should be managed by the people whose work created the service in the first place: frontline employees.* Given the right tools and a little training, frontline employees are quite capable of gathering information on their own performance, putting it on a chart or graph, matching it against predetermined norms, and deciding whether or not an improvement effort is called for.

3. *Feedback should be immediate; that is, information should be collected and reported as soon after the service is rendered as possible.* The sooner feedback is received by the people it concerns, the easier it is for them to take action.

4. *Feedback should go to the person or team performing the job, not to the vice president in charge of boxes on surveys.* Obvious? Maybe. But check your current feedback practices. How long will it take for information gathered today to reach the people on your frontline team? Rule of thumb: The older the data, the less useful for changing the way things get done in your service delivery system.

If Domino's and Pizza Hut can deliver direct, your feedback system can, too. Immediate, direct feedback helps your people meet their goals and targets, in the process minimizing the amount of "looking over their shoulder" corrective coaching you have to do.

5. *After it has served its immediate purpose, relevant feedback should go to all levels of the organization in a synthesized or aggregate fashion.* Everyone has a "need to know" when it comes to information about how the organization is performing.

6. *Feedback should be graphically displayed.* The adage that "one picture is worth a thousand words" is certainly relevant when it comes to feedback. A well-done graph can give employees both the big picture and a snapshot of specifics at the same time. It also provides a readily understandable comparative benchmark for the next batch of information.

Troubleshooting Your Display Feedback System

When a feedback system doesn't work, the reason can be that the information gathered is being used incorrectly. It has stopped being feedback and has become a chore, a threat, or something to be avoided. Dr. Karen Brethower, an industrial psychologist, uses the following five questions for troubleshooting a sick feedback system:*

*Chip R. Bell and Ron Zemke, *Managing Knock Your Socks Off Service* (New York: AMACOM Books, 1992, pp. 178–179).

1. *Is the feedback being used to embarrass, punish, or scold employees?*

> "You've all done well, except Charlene. Charlene, you're 20 percent below standard and dragging down the team."

2. *Is the feedback about something that has no payoff or relevance for the people receiving the information?* Support people may not be able to influence or assist salespeople with first-time sales.

3. *Is the information being provided too late for employees to act on it?*

> "Charlene, I just received the results from the customer satisfaction survey we did eight months ago."

4. *Is the feedback about something the people receiving it cannot change or affect?*

> "Customers are upset about the rising cost of paper."

5. *Is the information difficult to collect and record?* If it routinely takes longer to fill out the tracking paperwork than it does to talk to the customer, the feedback system is out of balance.

Interpersonal Feedback

Say "interpersonal feedback" to most people and they think of the last time they sat in their boss's office and listened as he or she droned on about the numbers on a printed performance appraisal form. That's not what we mean. Interpersonal feedback is a face-to-face, manager-to-employee conversation that is indispensable to an employee's morale, improvement, and growth. Like "display" feedback, interpersonal feedback comes in a variety of forms.

Some face-to-face exchanges will be based on your *opinion, expertise, or point of view* regarding the employee's performance.

> "Charlie, I can see you are working very hard to succeed. Can we talk about some things I think might increase your efficiency even more?"

Some exchanges will be based on *standards*, more formal measures and efforts that define quality performance.

"Charlie, I've been watching your calls per hour, and you've been improving steadily. Can we talk about how you can reach that standard more regularly?"

Standards, in turn, come in different styles. They can be:

- Written policies or rules—"Speed limit: 55 mph"
- Unwritten but generally accepted norms—"No swimsuits worn to the office"

Standards are the "rules of the road" that you discuss with new employees on Day One, so that they know what is expected of them on the job.

Whenever possible, coach from performance standards. Those are agreed on up front and are well known to your employees. You can't compel your employees to copy your style of dealing with customers, or to even respect your expertise—although they usually will. Employees tend to be more receptive to coaching based on concrete standards rather than on opinion and personal preferences.

Feedback is the breakfast, lunch, and dinner of champions because it feeds growth and success. Winners like to hear plenty of "You're the greatest" confirming feedback, and they love to see their progress tangibly recorded.

Questioning

Dorothy Leeds, author of *Smart Questions* (McGraw-Hill, 1987) says that:

> "People remember best those things they discover, learn, and experience themselves. If you want someone to digest and remember something, he has to think of it himself. The only way you help someone accept an idea as his own is to ask him a question and let him give the answer back to you."

Contrary to popular image, good coaches are askers as well as tellers. The best advice-givers most often are the best listeners. And good listeners are invariably good question-askers.

There are two types of questions: open-ended and closed. *Closed questions* such as "How many calls did you make?" or "What caused that complaint?" are great for capturing specific bits of information.

Open questions are generally more useful for coaching:

"What was she upset about?"
"What have you tried so far?"
"What would you like to accomplish when you call her back?"
"How might you plan your work more effectively?"

Open questions give the employee an opportunity to participate in the discussion, without feeling that he or she has been grilled like a suspect in a criminal case. There is a world of difference between being asked, "Did you do that?" or "Can you fix that?" and being asked, "What happened here?" or "How could that be fixed?" Good open-ended questions help the employee think through his or her problems and find the best solutions to them. And as you well know from your own experience, finding a solution yourself is a lot more motivating than having one spoon-fed to you.

There are a few more nuances to asking good coaching questions than simply asking open-ended questions, however. Avoid asking questions you obviously know the answers to—they come off more as courtroom-style accusations than as questions. Questions like:

"You actually thought that was the way we do things around here?"

Most rhetorical questions are equally insulting and unproductive.

Feeling questions are a good alternative to "What do you think?" questions, and they help clarify. Asking Charlie, "What might work?" is really only half the question. When Charlie has reacted with some possible solutions to the problem, ask, "How do you *feel* about these alternatives?" Then you're positioned to evaluate the possibilities as "partners" and reduce defensiveness.

"Why" questions can backfire on you. If you've ever been locked in a deadly game of "Why is the sky blue?" with a two-year-old, you know how irritating "why" can be. Better alternatives are, "Can you tell me more?" and "Can you give me some examples?" and "What do you have in mind?"

Leeds suggests ten open questions that (modified for the given situation) she finds to be versatile, future-oriented, and helpful in a number of work and life situations. Twisted a bit for coaching purposes, they are:

1. "What can I do to help?"
2. "What has to be done?"
3. "Can you explain how that might work?"
4. "How do you feel about that?"
5. "Can you say more about that?"
6. "How are you looking at that; what's your point of view here?"
7. "What are some reasons that may not have worked as well as you hoped?"
8. "What can you (we) change to make this work better?"
9. "What outcome were you (we) looking for?"
10. "What are you getting at there; can you be more direct?"

Listening Helps

There is, of course, more to questions than merely the asking. Listening to the answers helps. In fact, effective questioning involves several steps:

1. *Know why you are going to ask a question of the employee.* What is your purpose? What will you do with the information? If you are at risk of losing a good customer, then your discussion should center around that, not around Charlie's action—or inaction.

2. *Include information on your goal or concern when you position your question.* If you are to enfold the person in solving the problem you perceive, he or she needs to know how you see the problem.

> "Charlie, I had a call from Ms. Fizzlestick. She's been a very good customer over the years, and I'd like us to help her if we can. She was a little agitated by her last conversation with you. So I need to understand what this is all about. Could you recap the situation for me?"

3. *Listen to the response.* Nodding, taking notes, saying "uh huh," and the like, signal listening. Better yet, reflect—or play back to the employee—the important parts of what you hear to (a) be sure you've heard correctly, and (b) acknowledge that you've been listening.

> "In other words, Charlie, she didn't care much for our standard response to her request for more time. Do I have that right?"

4. *Reframe the problem.* Sometimes you can help Charlie work through the problem by simply changing perspective for him.

Coach: "How do you think she wanted you to respond?"
Charlie: "Well, she wanted more time to make the payment."
Coach: "What alternatives might she have been able to accept?"

5. *Propose action.* Once you and Charlie have explored options for the course of action, it's Charlie's turn to select the next step—with your help.

Coach: "It sounds like there are a couple of alternatives you can offer her. Which one do you want to propose first?"

It is natural to think first about lecturing performance problems out of existence. Natural, but ineffective. Asking quality questions expands comprehension and cooperation and increases the effectiveness of your people and their solutions to customer problems.

Informing and Instructing

Even the best, most thoroughly trained employee will need some straight-ahead help from time to time. Procedural changes, seldom used and poorly remembered protocols, new product nuances, and odd twists on familiar themes can stump even the most experienced, seasoned, bright employee. The keys to coach-as-instructor are logic, patience, and practice . . . and a system.

Step 1: Assessment. Instruction begins with assessment. Performance errors—as we pointed out in the last chapter—can come about for many reasons. Lack of skill and knowledge are but two. Assume, however, that you *have* eliminated other possibilities, and you are pretty sure that Charlie either never knew or has forgotten how to run a diagnostic on the Flying Squirrel word processing software program. In this instance, then, assessment means asking:

> "Charlie, which parts of the diagnostic are you having trouble with?"

Now you know what to emphasize in your instruction.

Step 2: Demonstration. People learn by watching, asking questions, and then practicing what they've seen others do. Give Charlie a positive example *and* some knowledge review.

Change places with Charlie; sit down at his workstation and perform the diagnostic. Hold a dialogue with Charlie as you go through the diagnostic for him. Begin with something like:

> "Let's start at the beginning, Charlie. What do you need to accomplish with a Flying Squirrel diagnostic?"

You then proceed through the procedure a step at a time, announcing what you are going to be doing, then demonstrating each step. The key to Charlie's learning the steps is remembering to point out how Charlie will recognize key points during the step and the signs that the step is complete.

> "Once you've entered a string of nines, you let the program run. That should take about 30 seconds. If it takes longer than a minute, there is probably a glitch. Write that down. You'll know the test is done when the green light stops flashing and the cursor reappears."

At the end of each step you demonstrate, have Charlie talk through what he just saw you do.

Step 3: Practice. Now it's Charlie's turn. Change places with Charlie, and have him walk you through the steps. You might start the practice by asking:

> "Okay, Charlie. Your turn. What do you do first? Talk me through it. Then show me."

Your most important roles at this point are (1) making sure that Charlie is getting the step right, and (2) giving Charlie positive feedback when he does so.

> "That was very good. Now you're ready for Step 2. What do you need to do to get Step 2 started?"

You should walk Charlie through each practice step until you are satisfied that he has mastered (or remembered) the step *and* any significant variations.

Step 4: Performance. If you have been instructing Charlie "off-line," it is time to move back to live work. If live work is more complicated than the practice you have been able to arrange, you should stay with Charlie for as long as it takes to confirm that he can make the transition. You may need to continue explaining nuances in the live work for a little while, as well.

Once you have decided that Charlie can work without your close supervision, you need to (1) designate the person Charlie should go to if he needs additional help, and (2) plan to check back with Charlie over the course of the day to observe and answer questions that have arisen.

Rule of thumb. If the procedure, process, or technique you need Charlie to master takes more than twenty to thirty minutes to learn, then you should go completely off-line with your instruction.

Every employee needs reinstruction in something at some time. That includes you. Asking a seasoned, experienced employee to teach *you* something new or to refresh you on a procedure or process sets a good example for an open listening environment.

Providing Positive Reinforcement

''Catch somebody doing something right today'' is an admonition that succinctly captures years of managerial wisdom, and it has special meaning and import for the service management effort. If you want people on your team to think and act in customer-oriented ways, seek out ways to catch them doing just that, and reward and recognize them for making the effort.

The biggest problem, of course, is that in the modern service workplace, most managers seldom see more than a small sample of employee behavior, and therefore they have few opportunities to personally catch employees, particularly frontline employees, doing anything—good, bad, or indifferent. You have to be prepared to use what you see, as well as find ways to see more.

Effective recognition and reward oil the wheels of willing cooperation and dedication to the job.

> *Reward* typically connotes money: salary and bonuses, cash awards, financial incentives, and other tangible payoffs in lieu of cash (though often chosen and presented in terms of their cash value).
>
> *Recognition* is typically less tangible, given for taking a little extra time with a customer, for going a step beyond nomi-

nal expectations, for caring about what the customer needs and expects to be done, and for looking for ways to do it better, faster, smarter.

Recognition and reward come in as many styles as there are recognizers and rewarders. Common approaches include:

- *High-profile formal.* Programs such as "Lightning Strikes" (IBM), "Bravo Zulu" (Federal Express), "Count on Me" (Southern Bell), "Great Performers" (American Express), and "Thumbs Up" (Citicorp Savings) come complete with detailed rules and objectives that everyone learns, and established prizes, payoffs, and awards that everyone can strive for.
- *Low-profile formal.* Little rewards can be as effective as big ones if they are used in the right way. Lapel-style pins and special name tags are practices used by service leaders such as First Federal/Osceola, LensCrafters, Citicorp, and Federal Express. At Citicorp Retail Service in Denver, good suggestions for new or better ways to serve customers warrant a "Bright Ideas" coffee mug or similar keepsake. The employee who submits the month's best idea wins a circulating trophy—a three-foot-high light bulb.
- *Informal.* A simple "thank you for your effort" note or a verbal "well done" delivered in front of coworkers (or in private) is a great way of recognizing people. Style counts every bit as much as substance. A handwritten note from the CEO saying nothing more elaborate than "I really appreciate the extra effort you expended making the senior officers' conference a success" is often more powerful—and certainly more lasting—than cash on the barrelhead. It's the sincerity and acknowledgment that count the most to the recipient.

Lasting Value

Sometimes recognition and reward programs take on dimensions that show you just how valued they can be to employees. At a theme park we worked with several years ago, we found a variety of clever ways to put feedback and recognition into the workaday life of employees—and improve customer satisfaction in the process. On the reward and recognize side, we started giving supervisors little cards called "Warm Fuzzies" to give to employees (you guessed it) caught "doing something good." Token givers were encouraged to write notes on the backs of the cards explaining what the receiver had done to merit a Warm Fuzzie. Four years later, we had supervisors giving out Warm Fuzzies, guests giving out Warm Fuzzies, and frontline employees giving Warm Fuzzies to one another, as well as to supervisors and staff support people.

We encountered only one problem with the system: hoarding. Not by the givers. By the recipients. Those "Warm Fuzzy" cards had point values—accumulated points could be redeemed for gifts and merchandise. But employees were not turning in the "Fuzzies" for the prizes. An employee focus group told us why. The psychological value of receiving the little cards outweighed the value of the prizes to many of the employees. As one employee put it, "When I'm having a bad day, I take out my stack of Warm Fuzzies and reread the notes on the backs, the nice things people said about me, and I feel better. That's more important than any prize I could buy for turning the cards in."

The solution here was easy: Give the employees credit for the points and let them keep the cards. (It made a mess of our research, but it worked.) The lesson was a big one: It's terribly easy to lose sight of how powerful a simple but sincere "You did a good job—thanks" can be.

"Respect for the dignity of our people demands that we answer some simple and universal questions:

What do you expect of me?
What's in it for me?
Where do I go with a problem?"

—Fred Smith
Federal Express

3

"Welcome to the Team!" Coaching the New Employee

''An employee is never more focused, malleable, and teachable than the first day on the job.''

—Horst Schulze
CEO, Ritz-Carlton Hotels

Learning is a way of life in Knock Your Socks Off Service companies, and it begins on Day One. In the past, new employee training often consisted of nothing more than a manager's telling the newbie, "Watch John for a few hours, then I'll turn you loose on the customers." If employees made some little mistakes during their first few weeks, well, customers understood about breaking in new help, didn't they?

Today, that informal approach to bringing new employees onboard is intolerable and untenable. Just as untenable is the likelihood that a fully skilled job candidate will walk in off the street ready and able—particularly able—to start tomorrow. The methods, policies, and procedures in your company or department are unique. So is the way you want customers treated. As for asking your customers to tolerate on-the-job trainee mistakes, forget that—unless, of course, you take a perverse pleasure in watching customers defect to the competition.

33

Getting Off on the Right Foot

Today, we need new employees to have more than just the right technical skills. We need them to also have great customer-handling skills, we need them to understand the company's views on customer care, we need them to know what they are expected to do when things go wrong for a customer (or a fellow employee), and we need them to know that their success is important to us. In short, we need them to know a lot about a lot, and learn it all in a hurry.

That can be overwhelming. To make it all happen, you need to have in place a plan for *welcoming, orienting, training,* and *transitioning* the new employee to the job.

Two respected industrial psychologists, Dr. Kenneth N. Wexley of Michigan State University and Dr. Gary P. Latham of the University of Washington at Seattle, have found that the way new employees are oriented and socialized contributes significantly to (1) the time it takes them to become effective on the job,

(2) their satisfaction with the job, and (3) the length of time they will stay with the company.* Several companies have validated Wexley and Latham's contentions:

- A three-year study at Corning Glass Works in Corning, New York, found that employees who went through a structured, supervisor-led new employee orientation process had a 69 percent lower turnover rate than employees who did not go through the process.
- A two-year study at Texas Instruments Inc. in Dallas, Texas, demonstrated that the time required for new employees to reach full productivity shrank from five months to three months for employees who had been carefully oriented to the company in general, and to their jobs and departments in particular.

The Disney Approach

One of the best-known examples of a highly focused, effective new employee orientation process is in place at Disneyland and Walt Disney World. Every new employee who goes to work at ''the park'' goes through the company's two-day Traditions course, whether that employee will be wearing a badge that says Guest Relations or simply operating a broom. The primary purpose of the seminar is to provide cast members with a firm understanding of corporate traditions and values, and to enfold them in Disney lore, language, and culture. It also provides generic skills essential to job performance—primarily basic information-giving and customer relations skills.

The Traditions seminar focuses on the big picture at Disney, while individual departments and units provide orientation in specific skills and detailed job performance information. At the Future World unit of Epcot Center, for example, trainers and lead employees conduct a five-day orientation and training program for newcomers. This program deals with everything from

*Kenneth N. Wexley and Gary P. Latham, *Developing and Training Human Resources in Organizations* (Glenview, Ill.: Scott Foresman, 1981).

the philosophy and purpose of Epcot and Future World to job skills, dress, and guest courtesy. New employees work side by side with a trainer until they are deemed ready to be "on stage" alone.

You don't have to be a Fortune 500 company or have a Disney University at your beck and call to create an effective new employee orientation process. As Professors Wexley and Latham's research and the experiments at Corning and TI confirm, the most critical parts of the new employee orientation are *you* and the four-step process of:

- *Welcoming* the new employee
- *Orienting* the new employee to the company and the job
- *Training* the new employee in the skills, attitudes, and expectations of the job
- *Transitioning* the new employee from trainee to fully functioning, successful professional

Step 1: Welcoming

What happens on Day One tells the employee a lot about the company, about the job, and about you, the coach. Marsha J. Hyatt, formerly of Minnegasco Gas Company, Minneapolis, Minnesota, tells this story about her first day on a new job:

> "I was all set to make a great first impression. I had really gone after this job, and I felt great when I got it. I arrived bright and early, only to find that the boss and all my peers were off on a project, and the person who had been assigned to show me around had decided to sleep in instead. The department secretary had no idea where my office was supposed to be—or that I had been hired. I couldn't even find any desk supplies. It was a grim first day."

If we believe that employees treat customers the way they themselves are treated, then isn't it critical that we be as careful about the first impression we make on new employees as we expect them to be about the first impressions they make on customers? What impression do you make on new employees if you leave them sitting in the lobby for half an hour when they report in? And if you aren't even there on Day One, what does that tell the employees about your dependability as a coach? What values do you communicate if you are there, but only have time to swoop down on the lobby, rush the new person to a desk, hand him or her an employee manual and a box of no. 2 pencils, blurt out a ninety-second lecturette on using the phone system, then bolt off for ''an important meeting''? One thing is for sure: Your actions aren't saying, ''Welcome to the team! I'm really glad you're going to be with us. I really want you to succeed.''

Regardless of how hiring is done in your organization, you will be well advised to put some time and thought into welcoming and orienting of the new employee. Create a checklist to ensure that you make the most of Day One. Many of the topics covered in this chapter should go on your checklist, but above all else, three things need to be there:

1. *Clear your calendar.* Plan to spend one to two hours with the new employee at the beginning of Day One. Also plan to spend an hour at the *end* of Day One discussing what the employee has done and seen, and answering more questions.

Do not *delegate first contact to a surrogate.* Gordon Shea, a Beltsville, Maryland, consultant who specializes in new employee orientation, emphasizes that, ''The new person is most concerned about the job and the immediate supervisor. It is a one-time opportunity to make a positive impression on the new employee.''*

2. *Alert the ''buddy.''* If you plan to use a buddy system to bring the new employee along, be sure that the buddy will be available on Day One and that he or she has time to prepare to work with the new employee.

3. *Alert the department.* Let people know that a new employee is joining the team and where the employee will be sta-

*Gordon F. Shea, *The New Employee: Developing a Productive Human Resource* (Reading, Mass.: Addison-Wesley, 1981).

tioned, and encourage all hands to introduce themselves and welcome the newcomer. Just as a newcomer can be unsettled by a room full of people staring at him as if he were a sudden arrival from Mars, coworkers can be put off by the sudden arrival of someone they have never seen before.

Step 2: Orientation

Many companies, such as Disney, Corning, and Texas Instruments, have a formal new employee orientation process designed to communicate relevant information to all new hires. But in most cases, new employees can't be exposed to the corporate message right away. Even if there *is* a program that is available immediately, it is up to the supervisor/coach to create the fit between the employee and the specific job assignment and department.

Once introductions have been made and the preliminary settling-in and housekeeping details have been previewed, the two most important orienting actions for the coach to take are *listening to the employee* and *discussing mutual expectations.*

Listening to the New Employee

It is important that you model your coaching style in this first meeting. Something simple will get the ball rolling:

> "Charlene, I've really been looking forward to having you here. I know a new job and a new company can raise a lot of questions. It's been ten days since we talked at any length. What questions do you have about the job, the department, the hours, anything that you've been wondering about since our interview?"

The point is to demonstrate your willingness to listen, to answer questions, and to be helpful to the employee. You want the employee to know that you aren't Attila the Awful. New employees are frequently reluctant to ask questions of a supervisor on Day One, but it is nonetheless important that you offer.

At Texas Instruments, it was found that discussions about the "real ropes" of how things worked at TI were highly praised by new employees. Your second goal is to ease the employee into the work scene, and avoid confusion and anxiety.

The Expectations Discussion

The expectations discussion should be just that: a frank discussion about your expectations of the employee and the employee's expectations of you, the job, and the company. Giving the employee an opportunity to express his or her expectations makes for a fuller, more complete orientation, and furthers the cause of smooth operating relations. It establishes you, the coach, as someone interested in dialogue with employees.

The Agenda

Three types of items should be on your expectation discussion agenda: *nitty-gritties,* or operational rules and expectations; *performance standards,* composed of process and outcome expectations of working with customers, colleagues, and other departments; and *your role* as the coach of the team.

Your nitty-gritty discussion items list should include, but not be limited to:

- The work day—hours, promptness, breaks, lunch, timekeeping
- Dress and decorum—how people work together, dress code, and policy
- General policies—attendance and absence, notifications
- Pay and benefits—where, when, and how much

Your performance standards discussion list should include, but not be limited to:

- Department mission, goals, and values
- Accountabilities and outcomes of the job

- How—and how often—the employee's work will be formally evaluated and measured
- "Hard" performance goals vs. "soft" performance goals

Your coach's role discussion items list should include, but not be limited to:

- How you and your employee will keep in touch about job performance
- The nature of your availability (Do you hold weekly meetings? Are drop-ins OK?)
- Your approach to managing (How formal/informal are you about reviews, assignments, etc?)

Expectation discussions can be enhanced by written materials. Ritz-Carlton Hotels, for instance, has a laminated, pocket-sized written expectations guide that managers refer to when discussing performance expectations and when doing refresher training with Ritz-Carlton employees. Such handy expectations summaries do not preclude an expectations discussion, but make useful reminders of them for employee and coach alike.

Step 3: Training

Nothing good happens for your customers until a member of your team makes it happen. Whether those employees are meeting face-to-face with customers or worrying over customers' billing and accounting problems in the bowels of the organization, it is their skill and effort that make the difference between a Knock Your Socks Off Service organization and wishful thinking. Developing, honing, and keeping an edge on your people's skills makes good strategic sense.

According to one study, employees who receive formal job training reach "standard" performance levels faster (72 percent faster), create less waste (70 percent less), and are better at customer troubleshooting and problem solving (130 percent better) than employees who learn their jobs through the tried-and-true—and very inefficient—"sit by Sally and ask questions" ap-

proach. In addition, there is pretty good evidence that employees who receive a significant amount of training on a regular
basis—between twenty and forty hours a year—stay with you
longer and receive higher marks in knowledge, skill, and hustle
from customers.

Training in What?

There are four kinds of skills your customer contact employees
need to do their jobs well: technical skills, interpersonal skills,
product and service knowledge, and customer knowledge. All
are critical to their success. Following are some tips for developing and honing these four crucial skill areas:

1. *Technical skills.*

- *Gadgets.* Frontliners need to learn to work not only your
  computer system but all of your office equipment. That
  includes the copier, fax, cash register (if you are a re-
  tailer), and telephones. Yes, telephones. Some of today's

systems would surely baffle Alexander Graham Bell. Assume nothing about a new employee's knowledge of
your systems. Even if the employee has worked with similar technology, he or she hasn't yet worked with your
particular variation. What employees don't know can kill
you with customers.

- *Paperwork.* They need to understand the purpose of your
  paper records and systems, not just which blanks to fill in
  with what letters and numbers. Any time paper affects
  the speed, reliability, and personal attention provided to
  customers, your people definitely need to know your
  forms and procedures cold.

2. *Interpersonal skills.*

- *People skills.* You hired your service people for their
  proven abilities to listen, understand, communicate, and
  relate with customers, as well as their technical and product skills. But no matter how good their specific skills may
  be, the more practice, the more training, the more knowledge, and the more experience you can give your frontline people, the stronger their skills will become. The
  burden needn't fall on you alone. A wide variety of
  books, videotapes, audiotapes, and low-cost seminars exists to remediate poor skills and polish competent ones
  toward excellence.

- *Self-assessment.* Give your people a mirror in which to
  view their current performance levels. Encourage employees who deal with customers over the phone to record several conversations and evaluate them alone, or
  with the help of others. Use videotaped role-plays to let
  them see themselves as others see them. Pass along customer comments, the results of mystery shops.

- *Teamwork.* With a little training in the proper way to give
  another person feedback (see Chapter 9), coworkers can
  help one another brush up on person-to-person skills. Do
  not, however, make this a requirement unless you are
  working in a peer team or "leaderless" team mode in
  your department. People are generally apprehensive
  about receiving a job skills critique, especially when there

is a possibility that the news will be less than thrilling. It is a tough spot to put a peer or pal in. The secret is to separate performance from person. Focusing on the former builds skills. Concentrating on the latter tears down self-esteem.

3. *Product and service knowledge.*

- *Technical aspects.* Customers expect your employees to know more about the products and services you sell than they themselves, as customers, do.
- *Competitive aspects.* Customers also expect your frontliners to know something about the products and services your competitors sell. The more knowledge and factual information (as opposed to sales hype) they can give your customers, the less need your customers will feel for comparison shopping.

4. *Customer knowledge.*

- *Customer profiles.* Your customer contact people in particular can never know too much about their customers, whether that involves the personal tastes of a consumer or the products and services of a business-to-business client. Your frontliners should be helped to develop a "style" for asking questions about customers—and write down what they learn. Customers expect your people to "stay told" about their specific tastes and buying patterns.
- *Heavy hitters.* Encourage customer contact people to create files on each of their five best customers, with notes on what they've learned about them. What do they notice about these best customers that is different from other customers? Would nurturing those traits build business as well as customer loyalty?

Where Training Comes From

If your organization has a training department that delivers the type of training your employees need, that's a big plus. But that doesn't mean you're free to give the responsibility to someone else and wash your hands of involvement. You need to ensure that the right skills are taught and that they are applied correctly on the job.

If you are in a small company, or one with no employee training department or system, you are de facto the training director, administrator, and instructor all rolled into one. You can, of course, pass some of the tasks to a senior or lead employee. But remember, training is too important to be done poorly or by people who don't want the responsibility. You and/or your trainer designate will need to learn how to do effective job instruction training. A community or junior college or vocational/technical school can provide you with such training or refer you to another institution for help.

Step 4: Transitioning

When Training Is On-the-Job

If your new employee training is done on-the-job (OJT), you need to plan the transition from training session to live, full-fidelity work carefully. Here are the factors to take into consideration and manage:

- *Most jobs have both simple and complex aspects.* You will want to move the employee from simple to complex work, but only as the simpler routines and processes are fully mastered. Even when the more complex aspects of the work are learned, the nuances and variations on complex cases, transactions, etc., will need support from a senior teammate or from you, the coach.

- *Handling live work is different from handling practice work.* It is even different from handling live work while sitting next to a trainer or "buddy." Anyone who has ever flown solo in an airplane or walked up to the first tee for the first time can attest to this: Flying with an instructor in the next seat or hitting balls on the driving range is very different from going "live." Job aids and checklists are invaluable help during the transition.

- *As a coach, you will be tempted to look over the newcomer's shoulder* when he or she goes live for the first time. Don't do it. Yes, keep an eye peeled for disaster, but let the employee establish a balance and rhythm to handling live work before you start giving feedback. Let the employee get her or his "sea legs" before you start coaching. If you start critiquing at contact number one, the employee will never establish the self-confidence to become self-correcting and self-supporting.

When Formal Training Is Available

Some organizations have their own in-company training groups that provide new employee skill training. The Disney organization, Motorola, Harley-Davidson, and McDonald's all have their own "universities" that teach both beginning and advanced job skills. Many organizations have begun delivering employee training via computer, where the training content comes to the employee through a desktop terminal. Some organizations provide technical and company-specific job training in-house, but send employees off to community colleges, universities, public seminars, and association conferences for customer relations skills and advanced technical training. Whatever the combination of training delivery methods you have at hand, you need to take some very specific actions to ensure that (1) training transfers to the job, and (2) you get the most return you can for your training dollar.

Here are two things you can do to make sure employees you *send off* to training get the most out of the experience.

1. *Hold a pretraining "heart-to-heart" expectations talk.* Sit down with the employee and discuss your expectations of the training and of his or her participation. Specifically, discuss:

- What the training will cover
- Why the individual employee is going
- Why the training is important to the organization
- Your assessment of the employee's strengths and weaknesses as they relate to the content and objectives of the training

- How you will help the employee apply the new skill or knowledge when he or she returns from training

2. *Assign pretraining homework.* The last thing an employee who is scurrying to make plans for a two- or three-day absence from the job needs is homework. Just the same, short preparatory readings, data gathering, worksheet preparation, and other training-related tasks can prime and focus the employee for the experience to come.

Welcome Them Back—and Help Them Apply What They've Learned

The training experience may have been great, the time spent highly productive, and the interlude just what the doctor ordered. But if the skill and information aren't quickly utilized "back on the job," the momentum will die. This is the single biggest reason, in fact, why training doesn't "take."

Here are three things you can do to *help smooth the transition* from classroom to real-world performance.

1. *Debrief them when they return.* It may seem as if we are recommending a lot of chatting. We are. Letting people talk about the new ideas, approaches, and skills they have been exposed to helps the training "transfer" to the workplace while reinforcing the value you put on the insights they've gained.

The discussion should be more than a friendly chat, however. It should be fairly detailed, and questions such as, "How do you think we can use that here?" should play a big part. Let your people show you that they have indeed come back with something new and useful. Be lavish in your praise of the new learning and ideas, and the effort the employee has put forth.

2. *Hold a skill drill or practice session for the newly trained.* We learn best by doing, but actual skill practice may be at a minimum in classroom training programs because of the number of participants, the style of the presenter, or the inability to address specific concerns in a general session. If it is important to turn the new learning into strong habits of performance, then the sooner the effort starts, the better.

3. *Catch them doing something new—and thank 'em for trying.* Making a new behavior an active part of an employee's skill vocabulary takes time and practice. It also takes feedback and encouragement. Particularly from you.

Nothing you will ever do in an employee's tenure with you matches the impact of what you do to bring that employee on-board gently and to make his or her first days comfortable, successful, and productive. As the twig is bent, so grows your coaching relationship.

> ''Setting and communicating the right expectations is the most important tool a manager has for imparting that elusive drive to the people he supervises.''
>
> —Andrew S. Grove
> CEO, Intel Group

4

"Nice Job, Charlene!" Coaching for High Performance

"People will often work harder for a title, special privilege, or plaque than they will for financial reward."

—Robert Conklin

We once heard a speech coach say that the three most important speeches for a student to study were not Lincoln's "Gettysburg Address," Winston Churchill's "Blood, Sweat, and Tears" or Marc Antony's "Friends, Romans, Countrymen" speeches. His

belief was that the most important speeches to study were the last speech the student *planned* to give, compared and contrasted with the speech he or she *actually gave*, compared and contrasted with the speech he or she *would give* if he or she could give the speech *over again*.

Translation: There is a lot to be learned from looking at our own experience—with a little help from the coach.

This truism is at the heart of coaching for high performance. It is a combination of ''catching somebody doing something right,'' targeted feedback, and leading through effective questioning.

Situation 1: Charlene's Big Presentation

Charlene has just made a presentation on the most frequent complaint of Acme, Inc., customers to an assembly of managers attending Acme's Fall Strategic Thinking Retreat and Golf Tournament. You helped her prepare, and she did an excellent job. In fact, factory manager Ralph Roughnready asked if Charlene could come make the same presentation to the operations people at his plant. This is a great time to both pass out positives *and* do some critical coaching with Charlene. So in the car on the way back to the customer service center, you start:

You: ''Charlene, you did a great job. All the hard work you put into studying the data and planning the presentation really paid off. Just a super job.''

Charlene: ''Yeah, that really went well—and the presentation stuff you put me through really paid off.''

You: ''I really like the way you talked about complaints as opportunities and said that everyone in customer service really appreciates how hard manufacturing works to make Zero Tolerance for Errors a reality. *Tell me, what did you like best about what you did?*''

Charlene: ''Well, I liked the parts you liked as well. But I really think that tying the customer suggestions to the quality process made a lot of sense to them and helped with the 'Not Invented Here' feelings.''

You: ''Yeah, that was good. Tell me, *if you were going to do it over again*—and if Ralph has his way, you probably will—*what would you do differently? What might you change?"*

Charlene: "Well—I'd change the way I present the data, and I might not go into as much detail next time."

You: "How would you get the information across without so much detail?"

Charlene: "Well, I think I might have fewer categories of complaints and suggestions. That would keep it from being so overwhelming as well."

You: "Makes sense. And it sounds good. *What do you need from me or the team* if Ralph decides to have you come talk with the factory operations people?"

Charlene: "Well, would a raise be out of the question?"

You: "Probably. But if you keep up this kind of work you could end up with my job."

Charlene: "Oh, great! Can I just walk from here?"

Situation 2: Then There's Charlie

Of course, not all your employees are "Charlenes"—ambitious, capable, and upward bound. There are a lot of "Charlies" out there—hoping to do a good job, pretty eager to please, willing to work hard for a fair day's pay, but a lot more interested in weekends than in Monday mornings. They need to be urged toward high performance as well. There are several things you can do to encourage individual customer service people to reach for higher performance.

Spot Incentives

Many service managers carry tokens of appreciation with them and pass them out when they overhear or receive a report of an employee going above and beyond for a customer, or simply managing to smile and be pleasant while handling a certified Customer From Hell.™ The key to making a spot incentive program work is focus. When you use spot incentives, be sure that you are clear with the employee about the reason for the award:

"Charlie, that was really good! I really like the way you rephrased what Mrs. Smith said to be sure you understood. That really decreases the chances of making a mistake.''

Spotlight the Performance

An employee who has done a good job or found an unusual or new way to serve a customer or solve a problem can profit doubly from explaining what he or she did to the rest of the team. Explaining one's good works or ideas to others can be rewarding and reinforcing—and it can give the employee an opportunity to articulate the key features of what he or she has done, thus solidifying it in the employee's *own* mind for future reference.

Caution

Some people would rather run naked through an Easter Parade than make a presentation to a group. A similar "beware" accompanies spot incentives. A service manager in Chicago tells of a service hero program run by her bank that included—as part of the top award—lunch with the president of the bank. A teller in our acquaintance's branch was one of a dozen tellers to be awarded the honor. The big day arrived and the teller was nowhere to be found, though she had clocked in for work. "I found her cowering in the restroom," our informant reported, "alternately feeling faint and throwing up. The idea of lunch with Jim the president—a really nice guy—wasn't a reward in her mind, it was practically a punishment."

Take Care in What You Assume About Other People's Motivations, and What They See as Rewarding.

Job Well Done

One of the best reward and recognition job aids we've seen is the forty-five ways to recognize people for a JWD (job well done) developed by Rosabeth Moss Kanter and her colleagues at Goodmeasure, Inc. We've listed them below to get you started.*

1. Create a "Best Accomplishments of the Year" booklet, and include everyone's picture and name, and a statement of each person's best achievement.
2. Name a space after an employee and put up a sign ("the Sissy Jones Corridor").
3. Briefly attend the first meeting of a special project team and express your appreciation for their involvement.
4. Show a personal interest in an employee's development and career after a special achievement, asking how you can help her or him take the next step.
5. Hold a luncheon meeting with project teams once they have interim findings. Express your appreciation. Encourage their continued energy. Provide the lunch.
6. Feature an employee of the month and not only put the

*"Holiday Gifts: Celebrating Employee Achievements," *Management Review* (December 1986).

employee's picture in a prominent place, but also honor him or her throughout the month at a series of lunches or other events. Make sure the employee and others know what the employee has done to deserve the designation.

7. Honor peers who have helped you by recognizing them at your (or their) staff meetings.

8. Nominate employees for any of the company's formal award programs.

9. Give employees copies of the latest management/business best-sellers or a subscription to a business journal.

10. Provide tickets to a sporting, musical, or cultural event (depending on the employee's preference).

11. Invite employees to your home for a special celebration, and recognize them in front of their colleagues and spouses.

12. Let employees attend meetings, committees, etc., in your place when you're not available.

13. Send a letter to every team member at the conclusion of their work, thanking them for their contribution.

14. Create a ''Good Tries'' booklet, and include innovations that didn't achieve their full potential, recognizing those who put in effort on the project. Be sure to include what was learned during the project so that this information can benefit others in the future.

15. Say hello to employees when you pass by their desks or pass them in the hall.

16. Have coffee or lunch with an employee or group of employees that you do not normally see.

17. Establish a place to display information, posters, pictures, and so on, thanking individual employees and their teams, and describing their contributions.

18. Say thanks to your boss, your peers, and your employees when they have done something well or have done something to help you.

19. When an employee or group presents an idea or suggestion, thank them, whether or not you will act on it. Thank them for their concern and initiative.

20. When discussing an employee's or group's ideas with

other people, peers or higher management, make sure that you give them credit.

21. When a current issue arises that is similar to one in which an employee has shown previous interest, involve that person in the discussion, analysis, and development of recommendations.

22. Give special assignments to people who have shown initiative.

23. Mention the outstanding work or idea brought to your attention by an employee during your staff meetings or at meetings with your peers and management.

24. Create group awards to recognize the outstanding teamwork of employees.

25. Get your employees' pictures in the company newspaper.

26. Write a "letter of praise" to employees to recognize their specific contributions and accomplishments; send a copy to your boss or higher managers and to the personnel department.

27. Ask an employee to help you with a project you consider to be especially difficult but that provides real challenge.

28. Send employees to special seminars, workshops, or meetings outside the company that cover topics they are especially interested in.

29. Present "State of the Place" reports to your employees periodically and acknowledge the work and contributions of individuals and groups.

30. Ask your boss to send a letter of acknowledgment or thanks to individuals or groups making significant contributions.

31. Introduce your peers and management to individuals and groups that have been making significant contributions, thereby acknowledging their work.

32. Ask your boss to attend a meeting with your employees in which you thank individuals and groups for their specific contributions.

33. Ask individuals and groups to be part of or make their

own presentations to higher management and to their own peers.

34. Create symbols of a team's work or effort (T-shirts or coffee cups with motto or logo, etc.).

35. Develop a ''behind the scenes'' award specifically for those whose actions are not usually in the limelight; make sure such awards are in the limelight.

36. Hold a raffle for members of an outstanding work group (give away a night on the town, a resort weekend, a home computer, etc.).

37. Send a group of employees or team on an outing (deep-sea fishing, baseball game, cruise, etc.) after completion of a project.

38. Recognize (and thank) people who recognize others. Make it clear that making everyone a hero is an important principle in your department.

39. Ask your employees themselves how you can best show your appreciation—what would they like?

40. Have an appreciation and welcome party whenever an employee leaves or joins your work unit.

41. Award personalized gifts (project team names printed on personalized T-shirts, rewards that recognize people's distinctive interests or hobbies, etc.) to all those involved with an innovation.

42. Take out an advertisement in an appropriate publication, thanking your employees.

43. Have the CEO or a very senior manager write a letter of thanks.

44. Provide a donation in the name of an employee to the charity of her or his choice.

45. Create an ongoing recognition award named after a particularly outstanding employee.

''I have yet to find the man, however exalted his station, who did not do better work and put forth greater effort under a spirit of approval than under a spirit of criticism.''

—Charles Schwab

5

"Can I Help?" Coaching on the Run

''What I don't need right now is a pep talk.''

—Don Shula

The made-for-TV movie version of coaching is a hoot. See the coach—invariably a man—stride confidently across the field. See the coach slap his hands and shout encouragement to his star player: "Way to go, Randy! Show 'em how it's done, son!" See the coach give a motivational lecturette to another player: "Look, Lyle, I know you can do better than that. Put your heart into it! Show some guts, boy!" Now watch as the coach takes on a Socratic role:

> "Billy Joe, what are you tryin' to do here, son? Which shoulder do you want down field, boy? Think, son, think. What are you tryin' to a-complish? Can someone here tell it to 'em?"

Very dramatic. Very dynamic.

And more than one corporate coach fancies him- or herself born of that same mold. Striding across the floor of his or her domain, passing out gold stars to the hot players, giving instant

and wise counsel to the faltering. Dynamic. Forceful. The image of self-assured mastery. And mostly a fantasy.

"Coaching on the run"—being able to spot real-time problems and intercede—is *useful* and *important*. But it is the exception, not the rule, of customer service coaching. And it is, more than anything else, a supportive, careful, inquisitive process. There is very little hand clapping, backslapping, or lecturing in a loud voice. And no making an example of Billy Joe for the others to "learn from." What they learn, invariably, is, when the coach is around, keep your head down and don't make any mistakes he can see.

Effective service coaches are alert for and sensitive to the sound of a transaction that has gone wrong—or is about to. And they do indeed intervene, help out, and even—on rare occasions—take over an explosive situation. The *vigilance* is continual, the *intercessions* only occasional.

Coaching on the Run . . . With Care

There are two broad steps for making the most of live, on-the-spot coaching situations.

Step 1: Observe First

It is easy to make a wrong assumption when you walk into the middle of a hot-sounding transaction. For instance, you over-hear Charlene talking on the telephone. "Look, Mrs. Smith," she is saying, "I've told you what I can do, and that's all I'm going to do." You wince, and your ears burn. Your next step should be to:

A. Put your hand over Charlene's mouth. She's done enough damage.
B. Grab the phone and explain that an escaped madwoman has been masquerading as one of your service represen-tatives.
C. Break the connection—and hope Mrs. Smith never calls back.
D. Hold a heart-to-heart talk with Charlene about her atti-tude problem.
E. None of the above.

If you *didn't* pick E, you haven't been paying attention. Here's the problem with climbing on your high horse and rush-ing to the rescue. Charlene may not even be talking to a cus-tomer. She could be exchanging jibes with her sister or mother-in-law. She could be defending herself against a bill collector. Or she could be dealing with a genuine Customer From Hell™ who has escalated the conversation beyond propriety. There is no way for you to know what transpired before you came on the scene, or what is happening on the other end of the line. Your only recourse: Stop, make your presence obvious, watch and lis-ten, and make it clear through your nonverbals that you are there, curious, and ready to jump in if Charlene needs help.

Note: You and your team should have a set of well-under-stood, worked-out nonverbal signals you use for asking for and offering others assistance with a tough customer situation.

Doing nothing is a hard rule to follow. Most managers pre-fer action to inaction. But unless the transaction you are watch-ing or listening to is totally out of control—pushing and shoving are occurring, screaming and shouting are ringing through the halls—your best option is to spend one minute, a full sixty seconds, watching, listening, and forming a sound hypothesis about what is going on before moving to Step 2, deciding what to do.

Step 2: Pick an Action

There are four actions to choose among in every Coaching on the Run situation. Each is dependent upon what you see and hear in Step 1, and on how "serious" you judge the situation to be.

Choice 1: Do Nothing

If, after sixty seconds of careful, obvious watching and listening, you come to the conclusion that the situation is under control or that what you thought you saw or heard is a nonproblem, then smile widely, nod—whatever it is you do to signal that you are moving on—and then walk off. Later, you might want to reassure the employee that you were just passing by and stopped to eavesdrop and see how things were going. You might, of course, even use the occasion to pass out a "Way to go, Charlene."

If you have any lingering doubts about the transaction you witnessed, you might ask: "Did you need some help there?" If the answer is no, take the employee's word for it and move on. You can, of course, use the occasion to remind the employee that asking for help is acceptable. "Good. Just remember, Charlene, anytime you think you need a hand with a tough customer, flash me the high sign and I'll step in. It's part of what I'm here for."

Choice 2: Wait and Discuss

If the conversation is not going in a way that is comfortable to you, but (1) you aren't sure that the transaction is offtrack, (2) the customer doesn't seem upset, and (3) the service rep isn't doing or suggesting anything you consider illegal, immoral, dangerous, or unethical to the customer, your best option is to stand back until the transaction finishes. Then, when an opening arises, take the employee aside—somewhere "offstage" if practical—and discuss the situation. Typical would be the Case of the Cranky Guest.

Situation 1: The Case of the Cranky Guest

You are the manager of a 350-room hotel that caters to frequent business travelers. Walking into the lobby from your office, you hear two members of the front desk staff—a good twenty feet away—saying rude and pointed things about a cranky guest. The lobby desk is such that sound, particularly conversation, can be heard well into the guest lounge area, a spot where guests regularly linger over free morning coffee after checking out.

You: "Charlie and Charlene, could you join me for a few minutes in the back? Gene can cover for us."

You **[after moving into your office and closing the door]:** "You may not be aware of it, but everything you say at the front desk can be heard all the way to the coffee area. Now, what was happening when I walked into the lobby?"

Charlie: "This Mr. Cranky really jumped all over Charlene when he checked out. He hollered about the towels and noise and the heat in the room—just a terrible display of bad behavior."

You: "And what did you do, Charlene?"

Charlene: "I apologized and wrote down his complaints and I comped his minibar bill. But all that barely slowed his mouth down."

You: "Well, I'm sorry the guy gave you such a hard time. You did a lot to try and calm him down. Can either of you think of anything you missed?"

Charlie: "I think Charlene did everything but give away the night. He's a regular, so I think we might follow up next week, and apologize again. Something like that."

You: "Good. Go for it. Now, I need to change the subject a little. I'm concerned that your postmortem could be heard all around the lobby. It's very easy for what we say to each other at the front desk to be overheard by guests."

Charlene: "I didn't even think about that—did you, Charlie?"

Charlie: "I sort of knew, but . . . "

You: "Glad you realized it. Just be careful, okay? If you need to vent a little, come back here where customers can't hear, all right?"

Choice 3: Interrupt the Employee

Sometimes an employee can become so engrossed in a transaction that he or she doesn't see a problem building, or see your signal that you are there to help, or realize that the problem is a simple confusion. At that point, it is acceptable to step in and change the momentum and direction of the discourse. The

Case of the Confused Software Buyer illustrates well the "interrupt-the-employee" approach.

Situation 2: The Case of the Confused Software Buyer

Charlie is on the sales floor, dealing with a customer who insists, "Windows™ version 6.0 allows you to transfer files from Mac to PC." Charlie explains that there isn't a Windows 6.0. The customer must be thinking of a different program. "Look," says the customer, "I oughta know, I use it every day at work." It's getting a little loud, and at least one other customer has noticed. You walk up, smile at the customer, then turn and address Charlie:

You: "Charlie, it sounds like there is some confusion here. May I help?"

Customer: "I'm trying to buy Windows 6.0, the one that lets you transfer files from Mac to PC. I use it at the office, but he says it doesn't exist."

You [addressing the customer, but keeping eye contact with Charlie, as well]: "Microsoft™ does have a Windows-based word processing program that does that—it's Word™ 6.0. Is that what you use at work?"

Customer: "Yeah, that's it."

You: "Charlie, could you show this gentleman where the Word™ 6.0 is?"

Charlie: "Oh, goodness. I'm sorry for the confusion. Let me show you where that's kept. I can give you some tips on installing it."

Your goal is to put some psychological space between Charlie and the customer so both can compose themselves. Directing your questions and attention toward Charlie gives the customer a chance not only to regroup, but to save face.

Note: You will want to explain later to Charlie that you heard the confusion, but didn't think there was anything to be gained—and maybe a sale to be lost—by pointing out the customer's mistake. If Charlie is new with you, you might also remind him that makes, models, names, and release numbers of software (or any product, for that matter) are easily confused by customers. It sometimes takes a little detective work to figure out what the customer is after and make the sale.

Choice 4: Interrupt the Customer

When the employee has clearly lost control of the situation and the customer (or the employee) is on a tear, it behooves you to interrupt and take over the situation. Be sure, however, that this is the only option left to you. Consider the Case of the Screaming Mimi.

Situation 3: The Case of the Screaming Mimi

The check-in lines are out the door. It always happens on pre-holiday Fridays. You staff up, and you warn everyone. You even precoach. But when half the world is trying to fly from point A to point B and the other half from B to A, things do get tense. You hear a loud voice coming from Charlene's station. You walk in that direction, and as you arrive, you see a customer shaking his fist at Charlene and hear him loudly demanding an upgrade from coach to first class. Charlene is alternating between beet red and very pale. She is avoiding eye contact with the customer and seems to have resigned herself to being yelled at.

You: "Sir, could you tell me what the problem is?"

Customer: "I called in a frequent flyer upgrade and this jerk insists I'm in coach. That's not acceptable."

You: "Mr. Gaul, I'm sure we can straighten this all out. Could you give me the information one step at a time?"

Customer: "Now look, I've been through this with her. I demand . . ."

You: "Sir, we will try to help you as best we can, but I need you to lower your voice a little and go through the problem with me. There are a lot of people flying today. About thirty of them are in line behind you

> right now. If you'll help us go through this step by
> step, we can figure out together what's gone wrong.
> Is that acceptable?"

Customer: "Just hurry up. I have to make that flight."

You: "Charlene, pull up Mr. Gaul's reservation so we can
> see what's going on here."

You have two objectives in a situation like this one. First, you want to get the customer back under control. When the employee has obviously given up, and the customer is hot, you must get the transaction back on track. That means your number-one goal is to regain control. Your second objective is to bring Charlene back into the land of the functioning, and into the transaction. You do *not*, however, want to release the transaction to her. There is too great a possibility that Mr. Gaul will start in on her again. You want him on his way. You should stay at Charlene's side through at least the next transaction. Depending on how seasoned she is and how shook she seems, you should at the very least start the next transaction and then bring Charlene into the transaction after you have greeted the next customer and started things off.

You: "Good afternoon, sir. What is your destination
> today?"

Customer [hands you his ticket]: "Chicago."

You: "Charlene, Mr. Mile is on flight 499. Could you pull
> that up, please?"

And from here, you can stop working and simply stand next to Charlene, perhaps chat with the customers, and observe Charlene to see how well she has recovered.

Later, when Charlene has a break or her shift ends, you will want to sit down with her, review the transaction, and be sure she is back on track. Your review should be a *short* reprise, simply going over the facts of the transaction. If Charlene is puzzled about how she could have handled the transaction better, move to the question-asking mode suggested in Chapter 6, "Help! I'm Stumped." If Charlene isn't terribly upset, and if the traffic on the floor is lighter than in this scenario, you can even do the postmortem right on the spot. But be careful about the amount of coaching you do in front of the customer and fellow employees.

> ``If (employees) make a wrong decision, that's something that can be corrected later. At least they acted in good faith. This is part of our commitment (to our customers).''
>
> —Isadore Sharp
> Chairman, Four Seasons Hotels

6

"Help! I'm Stumped." Coaching the Unsure Employee

''The whole idea behind productive coaching is to help people to solve their own problems. You cannot and should not solve the problem, or tell them how to solve it. You can, however, contribute, and you can make suggestions.''

—Dorothy Leeds

Any of us can find ourselves staring at an assignment, problem, or opportunity—without a clue. It may be that we don't see a connection between "it" and anything we've ever done, or even thought about before to any extent. The employee asking for help may be having a problem with a presentation, a particularly difficult customer, a new product variation, or simply a new level of challenge. Regardless, the best approach to coaching the unsure employee is through calm and careful questioning. Simply telling an employee how to deal with a problem—grafting your solution, however good it is, onto the employee and his or her problem—will decrease the employee's anxiety and solve the immediate problem, but it doesn't solve the employee's problem. What problem? The inability of the employee to think through and solve difficult or unusual problems.

Our view: *Solve the problem for the employee and that problem is solved, forever. Help the employee solve the problem, and a dozen future problems are solved as well.*

There are questions—and then there are questions. The first question to ask of a stumped employee isn't about the problem at all. It is, rather:

"How would you like me to help you?"

It is precipitous to dive into "who–what–when–where–why" with only the employee's call for assistance facing you. You need to know the *kind* of help the employee needs. The employee may simply need you to listen to his or her thoughts on the problem—to use you as a sounding board. The employee may need a fact, or a reference to someone familiar with some part of the task or problem at hand—a piece of your organizational know-how. Or the employee may need you to take on the role of Socrates and pull the answer out of his or her temporarily out-of-order thinking cap.

Twenty Questions—Abbreviated

There are four questions that can focus the process of helping the employee, without stifling his or her creativity.

1. *"What's the situation?"* Asking the employee to review the situation—the players, what has been tried, what has failed, who has said what, and when—gives the employee a chance to revisit the situation. It also helps you leapfrog the aggravating series of "Nope, we tried that" answers you get when you start tossing out standard, tried-and-true solutions before you actually understand what's going on.

You: "Charlie, your note said you wanted to discuss a problem with the Walters account. What can I do to help?"

Charlie: "Well, I'm not having any luck converting them from morning to afternoon pickups. And with the new schedule, we need them to accept P.M.s rather than A.M.s. What can I do that I haven't thought of?"

You: "Charlie, I'm not in the loop on the specifics. Would you mind going back a few pages and bringing me up to date?"

2. *"What do you want to accomplish?"* This is both an alignment question and a reminder question. You need to be aligned with the employee's goal for the situation, and the employee needs to be reminded that it is useful to know where he is going if he hopes to get beyond being stumped.

The answer you want is beyond the simple, "I want this jerk off my back." Though giving Charlie a chance to express that sort of sentiment is probably useful.

More helpful answers, however, will have to do with things like getting agreement on a problem resolution, helping a customer understand a policy decision, or clearing up a misunderstanding. You may need to re-ask the question in alternative ways to move the employee to clearly stating the outcome he wants.

You: "Charlie, what do you want to accomplish with Walters when you call him back?"
Charlie: "I want him to stop being a rockhead about this."
You: "Okay. But what do you want the situation to be at the end of your call? Where do you want things to be?"
Charlie: "Well, I want him to see the benefits of P.M. pickups and to agree to the 3:30 time."
You: "Is there a fallback or compromise situation we can be comfortable with?"
Charlie: "Well, we can slot him for later in the cycle. If he'd go with 4:30, anything up till 7:00 P.M., we could make that work."

3. *"What are your constraints?"* There are dozens of possible solutions to a problem, and hundreds of ways to resolve a situation with a customer. Only a few fit the constraints of customer preference, profit making, and company policy and procedure. Asking Charlie to name the limits he perceives to solving a confounding problem can be revealing. You learn a lot about what your customers are demanding and what Charlie perceives as the restrictions on his franchise to solve customer problems. Our experience: Employees see more barriers and constraints than actually exist. The result is that they rule out viable, even creative, solution options under the assumption that "Management would never go along with anything *this* crazy."

You: "Charlie, what are the constraints and parameters here? What limits are there on coming up with a pickup schedule that they'll go along with?"
Charlie: "Well, he's got to go along with P.M. pickups. And we've got to have his outbound either first or last on the truck."
You: "Why first or last only?"
Charlie: "Well, that's the way it's always come down from logistics . . . because of his load size, I guess."
You: "But is there a clear reason for that that we can point to and tell him about? One that he'll see the value of? Or is there any way to switch the routes around or put

him on someone else's route to make an A.M. pickup work?"

Charlie: "Gee. You've got me again. I'm going to have to ask logistics about that. I'll check that."

The point isn't to make Charlie feel dumb or to avoid solving the problem. The point is to help Charlie see solution possibilities other than the one that isn't working for him or his customer right now.

4. *"What do you find challenging?"* You need to narrow down Charlie's problem and find the element of the situation with which he is struggling. Getting a tight focus on a single element makes the problem more manageable for Charlie and gives you a better chance to give Charlie better help.

You: "Charlie, I know you've been working on this for a little while—what's the toughest part so far?"

or

You: "Charlie, I know you've handled problems similar to this in the past. Where do you see the challenge in this one?"

Not every "I'm stumped" is an opportune coaching-through-questioning moment. Sometimes you simply need to jog Charlie's memory.

Charlie: "I'm stumped on this return for credit memo. It's international—German—and has foreign exchange calculations with it."

You: "Didn't you have something like that last fall? It was Italy, not Germany, but the principle would be the same, wouldn't it?"

Charlie: "I forgot that one. Let me look it up."

The Hot Hand-Off Follow-Up

Sometimes the "I'm stumped" employee hasn't the luxury of consulting you and trying again. Sometimes the employee is face-to-face or mouth-to-ear with a customer, and needs you to solve the problem fast and do the coaching later. A good number of HMO, medical insurance, and software companies have a second tier of senior service reps in place to deal with rare or highly technical situations. These same ``Super-Troopers''* also act as back-up for the ``I'm stumped'' first-line reps on their team. They are in an ideal position to ``coach back'' after the problem is solved and the customer off the line.

You:	``Charlene, I've finished with Mrs. McChisler. And I think I've solved her problem. Let's go over this one, okay?''
Charlene:	``Sure. I'm lost with her case.''
You:	``Okay. What information did she give you up front?''
Charlene:	``Just her policy number and the refusal we sent her.''
You:	``Did she give you any history on why she wanted us to pay for her out-of-network procedure?''
Charlene:	``She claimed we did it before, but I couldn't find a record of that.''
You:	``Ah, that's it. Okay. Did she tell you how long ago that was?''
Charlene:	``Yeah. Eight years.''
You:	``What you probably didn't know was that she wasn't with us eight years ago. She was with Medlock, a company we bought.''
Charlene:	``Yeah, okay. So?''
You:	``Well, she's grandfathered for some of the old Medlock provisions, and you'd have to know that if she didn't tell you.    ``Do you have a list of companies we've acquired so that you can ask about that when the records don't go as far back as the customer does?''
Charlene:	``No, but obviously I could use one.''
You:	``Okay. Let me fax one to you and the team . . . ''

*And, of course, sometimes the Super-Trooper is you, the manager.

The principle is still the same. Asking questions brings Charlene out of the "I'm stumped" mode of thinking into the light of "I can do that after all." All Charlene was missing in this case was a little job aid, not some deep, dark customer-handling secret.

> ``It has been well said that the effective leader must know the meaning and master the technique of the educator.''
>
> —Selznick

7

"This Could Be Tricky."
Coaching
for Difficult Duty

*"Do everything in your power to help them
be as successful as possible.
You succeed only when they succeed."*

—Ferdinand F. Fournies

You know the feeling: the butterflies in your stomach, the sweat on your palms, the tick that develops above your left eyebrow, that all say "I am *not* looking forward to this." There are times when individuals on your team—and sometimes your entire team—must prepare to deal with difficult customer situations, situations that range from "tricky" and sensitive to those involving flaming, fire-breathing Customers From Hell™. Think Exxon Valdez and lawsuits over hot coffee on the one extreme and packaging problems on the other—as in, "Folks, the last 1,000 module 402's we shipped didn't have the operating instructions in the packing box." In these and a thousand possibilities in between, it's customer service that stands in the crosshairs of customer ire.

There are two kind of tricky situations you and your employees should work through and preplan before tackling:

- Single-customer disasters
- Marketwide missteps

Single-customer disasters. Some individual customer encounters are destined to be filled with tension, particularly those involving problems brought on by our own "goofs." It may be that a shipping mistake was made, a price was misquoted, or a product failed. It could even be that a customer willfully misunderstood, and is very upset with *you* for not getting it right anyway. These are those "Mr. Haversham is *not* going to like this" moments we all hate.

Marketwide missteps. These range in impact and importance from the fortune cookie factory that mistakenly packaged its special "adult" fortunes for regular restaurant distribution and the clothing catalogue publishers that inadvertently published a revealing photo in the men's underwear section to automotive safety recalls and reports of potentially fatal product tampering. In these situations, some customers will respond well. They will be, if not thrilled, at least understanding. Others become fire-breathing, job-threatening Customers From Hell™. Whatever the cause or however severe the result, marketwide missteps are the times when you know that the phones are going to light up like Las Vegas slot machines.

While the specifics will vary depending on whether you are coping with a single-customer incident or a massive business situation, the same four-step procedure will help your team individually and as a group survive the problem. The four steps are:

1. Talk through the situation.
2. Anticipate reactions and problem-solve.
3. Role-play.
4. Make contact with the customer.

Step 1: Talk through the situation. Taking time to talk through a tricky situation before it hits will give you the important ''who, what, where, when, and how'' background information you and your team will need in order to construct an effective response to the coming tumult of customer outcry. The questions in Figure 7-1 will help you guide such a discussion.

Step 2: Anticipate reactions and problem-solve. In some situations, the ''solution'' will be created for you by the legal depart-

Figure 7-1. Questions to help frame the situation.

- Who is (will be) involved in this tricky situation? One customer? Many customers?
- What happened? Or what will or may happen as a result of this situation?
- Who in your organization may need to play a role?
- When will or did the customer(s) learn about the situation?
- How will or did the customer(s) learn about it—from you, from their own experience, from the media?
- How will we contact the customer(s)? By phone? By letter? In person at our place of business? By going to the customer's home or business?
- Is the information the customer(s) has (have) at this moment accurate?
- How may the customer(s) react to this situation?

ment. In others, it will be up to you and your team to create the specific solution. You will need to generate the words to say, the recompense to offer, the explanations to give, and so on. In the latter situation, you will want to problem-solve with the employee or employees who will be involved in actually handling the tough situation.

While many situations call for customer involvement in developing final solutions, this step invites you to investigate the types of solutions that have worked in the past, and to create new solutions as appropriate. The questions in Figure 7-2 will help you lead your team—or even one individual—through a solution-building discussion.

Step 3: Role-play. Now it is time to help your team practice the actual customer encounter. *Without* this practice, the employee(s) will be as on edge and unsure as the customers. This is definitely a time when you want your people to be at their most competent and confident. If just one employee will be talking with customers, you may want to involve another team

Figure 7-2. Problem-solving questions.

- If the situation has happened before, what did that previous solution look like?
- What might the customer want to have happen to resolve this situation?
- What are we willing to do, invest, or spend to resolve this situation?
- Who should be involved in that decision making? The front-line employee? The manager? Senior management? A supplier or vendor? The customer?

member in this step, or take an active part in the role-play yourself. Problem solving allows employees to learn *about* possible solutions. Role-plays help them learn to *implement* them. Because role-plays are interactive, use them to:

- Try out wordings and explanations.
- Explore options.
- Understand the customer's emotional response to the situation.

Step 4: Make contact with the customer. Your employee, or your team, is now ready to handle the customer encounter. This may mean proactively contacting customers, or simply being ready when customers contact you.

One caution: Don't leave your employees dangling in the wind. At this point, some employees will be ready to go full steam ahead on their own. Others will still need your support. You may choose to join, or even take the lead, in talking to the customer with your employee in a single-customer situation. Whether on the phone or face-to-face, determine in advance which of you will take the lead. Sometimes the simple fact of your presence, ready to jump in if the situation warrants, will give an employee the confidence and comfort level he or she needs. When the situation is a companywide misstep, you may want to pair your more experienced employees with less experienced ones for the first few calls. And you will definitely want to designate several senior reps to take ''hand-offs'' from the newer, less seasoned service representatives. A product recall or emergency situation of any sort is a bad time for learning by doing.

Situation 1: The Case of the Tardy Title Search

Talk through the situation. Knowing that difficult duty is coming before it hits requires that you continually assess the current situation. You and your team need to be aware of what's happening to whom and how they may feel about it.

As manager of mortgage operations, you train your mortgage clerks to use a detailed checkoff system to ensure that all necessary paperwork is completed in time for a customer's closing. While the system is primarily there to prevent problems, it also helps employees spot mistakes that may have slipped through.

Two days before Mr. Haversham is scheduled to close on his dream home, Charlie comes to you.

Charlie: "I just reviewed the file and realized that the title search for Mr. Haversham's home was never ordered. This is going to cause a delay in closing. He doesn't know about this yet, but based on the encounters I've had with him so far, I know he's going to be livid."

At this moment, fixing blame for the error or even coaching Charlie on how to avoid this problem in the future comes second to preparing him to deal with the current situation. You can use the "framing" questions from Figure 7-1 to help you assess the current circumstances and prepare your action plan. Among the questions that you and Charlie will want to focus on in this particular situation are these three:

- Who besides Mr. Haversham is an important stakeholder in buying this property?
- What will or may happen if Mr. Haversham can't close on the scheduled date?
- How can Charlie reach Mr. Haversham to talk with him about this situation?

Problem-solve. The problem-solving questions from Figure 7-2 help you guide Charlie to an appropriate plan of action. Checking with other employees, Charlie learns that Totally Titles is willing to do rush searches, for a price. You okay the expenditure. Charlie contacts Totally Titles and learns that they can do the work, but it will take two days—delaying Mr. Haversham's close by one day. The technical problem now under control, you and Charlie can be about the business of anticipating Mr. Haversham's reaction to the delay and how you can best manage it.

Role-play. Because Charlie is very nervous about talking with Mr. Haversham, you suggest that he play the role of the customer first, while you play the role of the employee.

You [to Charlie]:   "As I explain the situation and ask for your cooperation and understanding, you respond as you think Mr. Haversham will respond. Say both the words you think he will say to you and how you think he feels about the situation and our company and you. Okay, Charlie?"

Then switch roles. Now that Charlie has seen the situation through Mr. Haversham's eyes, you let him practice his role in problem solving. Several times you stop the role-play to talk about what is happening, and what Charlie and Mr. Haversham may be feeling about the encounter. Perceptions and feelings— the subtext of the discussion—are often even more important than the specific words being spoken.

Make contact with the customer. You and Charlie agree that a joint conference call to Mr. Haversham is the best way to break the news. While Charlie will take the lead, your presence on the call will indicate to Mr. Haversham just how important, and unusual, the situation is. It will also allow you to take over the call if Mr. Haversham becomes volatile or Charlie starts to falter. You want to hold the conversation where you and Charlie can see each other so that you can communicate nonverbally, or even slip each other notes as you go.

Postmortem. It is important that you and Charlie review the follow-up steps that must be taken as a result of your conversation with Mr. Haversham. Once the steps from the end of the phone call to the closing have been written down and time-lined, you and Charlie can and should spend a few minutes doing a postmortem of the actual conversation with Haversham.

Address questions like:

"Charlie, how do you think that went?"

and

"Did anything happen during the call that we hadn't anticipated?"

and

"Was there anything in the call we hadn't prepared for?"

These will give Charlie—and you—an opportunity to learn from the problem and plan better the next time a "Mr. Haversham isn't going to like this" situation occurs.

Situation 2: The Case of the Icky Ice Cream

Acme Ice Cream Inc. is a major Midwest ice cream producer. Like all food processors and packagers, Acme has an elaborate food safety and quality assurance program. But some things are beyond the reach of the best organization's controls.

In this instance, a shipper's mistake has contaminated ingredients that go into Acme products, in such a way that quality assurance processes were unable to detect the problem until finished product had already been shipped. Your task is to prepare your customer service team to handle the flood of calls from concerned customers you will shortly face.

Talk through the situation. It's possible to predict, in a broad way, most of the "tricky" situations your team is likely to encounter in the normal course of doing business, from out-of-warranty returns, to product recalls, to computer crashes, to customer errors, to price increases, to . . . you name it. Many organizations today routinely preplan their approach to major potential missteps. At Acme, disaster recovery planning is regularly reviewed.

As part of the disaster recovery team at Acme Ice Cream, you have been continually looking to the future, anticipating the types of business situations and customer service incidents that might occur. You, in fact, have already participated in an exercise around the question:

> "What would happen if, heaven forbid, we had a product recall? Let's say a supplier delivered a contaminated ingredient that was mixed into a week's worth of our Vitally Vanilla ice cream?"

When the Centers for Disease Control calls to tell you that it's investigating an outbreak of salmonella and that the strongest link between cases is Acme's Vitally Vanilla ice cream, you are pre-prepared. With the team, you compare your "what-if" analysis to the specifics of this actual situation as related to you by the CDC.

Anticipate reactions and problem-solve. Your "what-if" analysis included developing a plan for handling the first twenty-four hours of the crisis. Unfortunately, even the best recovery planning will rarely take you beyond the first twenty-four hours of an actual situation. After twenty-four hours, the situation will take on its own unique elements. It will turn and twist in unexpected ways. The disaster recovery team will meet frequently to continually anticipate the reactions of customers, employees, and the media, and to update the action plan.

Because of the nature of the product recall situation—the unusually large number of customers affected, possible legal ramifications, the need to manage public perceptions, and the like—the action plan will be determined at the highest level and then cascaded down to the customer contact level. You hold a meeting with your customer contact team to let them know what happened and the current plan.

You: "At 4:30 P.M. yesterday, we learned that the Centers for Disease Control has linked our Vitally Vanilla product to an outbreak of salmonella. As you know, this is exactly the type of difficult situation for which we created the disaster recovery team. I've been meeting with the team all night, and here's how we need to proceed today."

In addition to telling your team what they will be expected to do for customers, you will also want to tell them how to deal with the media and with questions from family and friends, and then spend some time dealing with concerns that they personally may have.

You: "So, we'll be opening up a special 800 number consumer hot line. I'm looking for volunteers to work overtime so that we can get twenty-four-hour coverage on that line. In addition, you may receive calls from the media about this. I would like all media inquiries to be routed directly to me. We are going to do our best to keep you informed and updated. We'll be E-mailing you the latest information as we have it."

Note: A large part of the success of your problem solving in this situation will depend on recognizing that there are some tricky situations in which it is impossible to undo what's been done—or the public's perception that something has gone wrong. At those times, department-level planning is largely about helping your employees know how best to manage the incoming calls in a way that calms customer fears, deals forthrightly with the facts, and is seen as open and aboveboard.

Role-play. With a large team assigned to phone duty and little time for training, it's impractical for you to role-play with each service representative. But because the stakes are so high, you know that you must give your team some practice before putting them on the job.

Working in groups of ten to fifteen service representatives each, you ask employees to listen as two senior representatives role-play typical call situations. In one, Charlene pretends to be a customer who's calling because she heard about the outbreak on the news and wants a refund. In another, Charlie pretends to be a reporter looking for an inside scoop by calling on the 800 line.

You emphasize the best wordings and practices from each role-play, even writing down some key ''wordings that work'' on flip-chart paper and posting them in the consumer response phone area. As the teams work, you ask them to talk through every situation they can imagine encountering, and plan in detail for the most likely of those encounters.

Make contact with the customer. While Acme is working to proactively contact distributors and customers, through phone calls, site visits, express letters, and the media, your team is ready and waiting for calls to come in on the special 800 number. All representatives know that a supervisor will be available at all times to handle calls that escalate or raise issues outside of those the representatives have been prepared to handle.

> ''Employee involvement and ownership in developing solutions are vital to the coaching process.''
> —Steven Stowell and Matt M. Starcevich

8

"Great Opportunity, Charlie!" Coaching for Special Situations

''One of the things that a coach can do is to find out
what it is that intrinsically motivates people and
use that to help them reach personal or
group stretch goals.''

—Robert Hargrove

Growing your team members means giving them stretch assignments—opportunities to do new things, to experience new situations, to meet and work with customers and clients, vendors, senior managers, and in general to "go where they have never gone before."

But stretch opportunities aren't sink-or-swim assignments. They need to be matched to the skills, interests, and ambitions of your team members. So Step Zero is to know your people well. Who is pining to move ahead? Who would consider an "opportunity to stretch" a punishment in disguise? Who are the 9-to-5ers and who are the "go-anywhere–do-anything" go-getters? Who have you seen perform at the top of their game day in and day out? Who have you observed "stretching the envelope"—trying out new solutions and ways to do things on a regular basis? Who nags you for more resources and for permission to try out new ideas? Who keeps reminding you that they want a crack at a tougher, more challenging assignment?

Note: The phrase ''equal opportunity'' is germane here. You are obliged to offer growth opportunities to *all* satisfactorily performing employees. It's just like overtime. And like overtime, the law, and a good many labor contracts, requires you to spread the opportunity around. And like overtime, all are free to accept or decline—within limits.

What Constitutes a Growth Opportunity?

Anything can be a growth opportunity, as long as it helps the employee to gain new skills or to exercise his or her skills in a new, challenging way. Making a presentation to a customer or senior management or simply to the team can be a stretch opportunity. So can dealing with a vendor or visiting a customer's facility, or taking on a new, more difficult or challenging book of work.

Situation 1: The Senior Management Presentation

Step 1: Present the Opportunity. Let's say that senior management has asked for a review of customer complaint data, your complaint-handling system, and the estimated impact of your department's work on customer retention. Charlie has helped you from time to time with data assembly and analysis. And he has been candid about his ambitions. He wants to be seen as having management potential, not just as a senior customer service rep.

You: "Charlie, senior management asked me for a presentation on our complaint management system. You've worked on complaint data with me. How would you like to make part of the presentation?"

Step 2: Explain the Situation Carefully. This is a most critical step. Once Charlie hears and accepts your challenge, it is important to have a careful, detailed discussion of the objectives, desired outcomes, and parameters of the assignment.

Making a presentation to senior management may not be a big deal to you, but it could be—probably is—to Charlie. Without some pretty good input from you, Charlie could head off in some wrong directions, inadvertently making a nightmare of his big opportunity. Without your careful guidance at the outset of his preparation, Charlie could miss the mark completely.

You: "Charlie, our goal is to communicate three things: our complaint rate, our complaint-handling system, and our recovery success. I'd like them to also see how we contribute to overall customer retention. From past experience, we should count on thirty minutes, including a lot of give-and-take discussion."

Step 3: Solicit Participation in the Planning. At this point, it is important to draw Charlie into the thinking and planning. He has probably been sitting there taking notes, but you need his head, not just his writing hand, engaged in the task. You need his ideas, and you need to be sure he understands your goals and parameters.

You: "Charlie, what's your past experience been with this sort of presentation?"
Charlie: "Well, I made that presentation to the department on last year's data."
You: "That's good. What did you like about that presentation? What might be applicable here?"

After you've gotten a sense of what Charlie has done before and how he would approach this presentation, you need to (1) give him some insight into the group, and (2) set him a clear assignment.

You: "You've got some good ideas to build on, Charlie. Let me tell you a bit more about the group. First, these managers like data, but don't like to get bogged down in the details too much. They like to know trends and one or two pertinent examples. They tend to interrupt and ask questions. . . .

"I think that's enough to get us started, Charlie. The presentation is in two weeks. Would you be comfortable doing the first outline for us to go over—say, by Wednesday afternoon?"

Step 4: "Practice, Man, Practice." Once you and Charlie have agreed on the outline, split up tasks, and completed your draft materials, it's rehearsal time. Take the rehearsal in two parts. First, talk through the presentation—who will say what, followed by what, through to the end. The second part is to actually make the presentation, using a select departmental group as your audience. This serves several purposes: It gets Charlie on his feet in front of a group, it gets you both feedback from the team, and it gives the team information on the department.

Step 5: Postmortem. After you and Charlie have made the presentation to management (or Charlie has called on the customer, or dealt with the vendor, or spent Day One on his new

book of business), you want to give Charlie a chance to revisit—
positively—the assignment.

You: "Charlie, that obviously went well. What part did you
              like best?"

and/or

              "What part do you think they responded best to?"

and/or

              "What do you think had the most impact on them?"

Once you've walked Charlie through the Valley of the
Shadow of Death, and he's lived, he'll be back on your doorstep
with a backpack, looking for a repeat trip.

Situation 2: The Case of the Assistant Coach

Spring is coming. And with it, a flood of business for your
mail-order garden bulb business. You are going to be hiring
twice as many temps this season as last. Question: How in heck
are you going to get them up to speed?
Well, there's Charlene. For most of the winter, Charlene has
been the senior on-the-spot customer service person. On top of
that, she is an avid gardener. She knows her stuff. She knows it
so well that you took her to the West Coast Greenhouse Show
with your marketing team to help select new flowers for this
year's catalogue. She should be great—if she'll take the assignment.

You: "Charlene, we're going to be staffing up soon for the
              spring catalogue rush. It goes in the mail in three
              weeks. We need someone to train the new hires.
              How would you feel about taking on that assign-
              ment?"
Charlene: "Geez, I'm not a teacher. I've never much more than

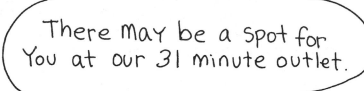

	taught Sunday School. Don't you need to be educated specially to do that?''
You:	''Well, I have done all the training in the past, so I can help you prepare. And the Gardening Wholesalers Association has a couple of teleselling courses we can use. Our selection is going to be just as careful as when I hired you, so we will be getting people with as close to your experience level as possible. And I will work with you on training the first seven or eight people we hire.''
Charlene:	''Well, I'd like to try, I really would. But, I'm not sure. . . . Okay, you talked me into it.''
You:	''Charlene, you went to several agricultural extension courses this winter, didn't you?''
Charlene:	''Well, sure. I do every winter.''
You:	''Okay. Let's start easy. Tomorrow I'll bring in the

	materials I've used in the past, you bring in your extension course material, and we'll see what we've got to work from."
Charlene:	"Okay. But I might need more help than you expect."
You:	"That's a good point. I have lots of confidence in you, though. Let's talk about that Sunday School experience. Tell me how you went about getting ready to teach there."
Charlene:	"Well, let's see. Oh, we had these lesson plans that came from the Synod . . . "

Note how the coach did a little selling but primarily stuck to our basic coaching for new opportunities outline:

Present the opportunity.

> "We're going to be staffing up soon. How would you feel about taking on the assignment?"

Explain the situation carefully.

> "I've done the training in the past. I'll work with you on training the first seven or eight new people."

Solicit participation in the planning.

> "Tomorrow let's go over the extension division materials from your winter course."

> "Let's talk about that Sunday School teaching experience."

As long as you bring your people through the new opportunity a step at a time, you can be sure you are creating a valuable resource for the future.

> ``Mentors (and coaches) do not give courage,
> they uncover courage.''
>
> —Chip Bell

9

The Coach's Nasty Nine

"Don doesn't care if they like him. That is not his job. His concern is that players be their best."

—Ken Blanchard on Don Shula

All coaching opportunities are *not* created equal. Some are a breeze to deal with—a delight, even. Especially those that focus on growth and positive performance. Others make you wish you'd gone into an easier line of work—something like minefield clearing or wild animal taming.

There are three kinds of coaching challenges service managers call their toughest coaching tasks. The first are *simple perform-*

ance adjustments: slumping sales, really long phone calls, mix-ups about rules and regulations. They need a sit-down discussion, a little thought, and a follow-up plan, but by and large their solutions are straightforward. The second set, *performance adjustments in complex times,* are adjustments that must be made but that can backfire because of complicating circumstances, like a labor shortage, a skill shortage, or the need to honor special employee or customer circumstances. A final group of tricky coaching situations are *trouble-on-the-team* problems: employees who aren't getting along, or who are afraid of change, or who have personal habits that are upsetting to the team or customer relations and harmony. Be advised: None of these are problems we consider intractable or that require warnings, documentation, or threats of sanction instead of coaching.

Each of the nasty nine coaching situations we cite comes from real life, and all of them can be tackled by applying a four-step coaching formula we call:

Dr. Tom's Sure-Fire Coaching Conference

Dr. Tom's technique (named after its creator, Dr. Thomas K. Connellan) is a four-step process for discussing performance problems with employees, peers, or associates. Used as both a planning guide and a discussion outline, it is an invaluable coaching tool.

Before you sit down to coach an employee through one of the Coach's Nasty Nine, you need to go through a quick mental checklist to be sure that the problem is indeed the employee's and not yours. If you can say, "Absolutely, positively, unequivocally, yes" to each of the following questions, you are ready for a face-to-face coaching conversation.

If you are unsure or hesitant to answer yes to any of these questions, you should, at the very least, keep your ears—and mind—open to the possibility that the problem is something you *share* with the employee. Go back and review the previous chapters in this book, especially Chapters 2, 3, and 4.

That important consideration out of the way, you are ready

1. Does the employee have a clear understanding of the expectations and standards for the job?   Y   ?   N
2. Does the employee have a clear understanding of the way you expect him or her to deal with customers?   Y   ?   N
3. Has the employee been fully trained in both the technical and the interpersonal parts of the job?   Y   ?   N
4. Does the employee regularly receive feedback on his or her job performance—both the technical and the customer relations aspects?   Y   ?   N
5. Does the employee regularly receive positive praise for good work, as well as "spot" coaching and support, when he or she takes on difficult tasks?   Y   ?   N
6. Does the employee clearly understand your views on teamwork, intradepartment cooperation, and collaboration with fellow employees?   Y   ?   N

to tackle the Coach's Nasty Nine using Dr. Tom's Sure-Fire Coaching Conference.

Dr. Tom's Sure-Fire Coaching Conference

Step 1: Position the Discussion

Positioning the discussion lets the employee know what you want to talk about and why. If you want to talk with Charlene about her new account opening rate, you might say:

> "Charlene, I'd like to sit down with you later today to talk about new account openings. I was going over the

latest Openings Report, and I see you're not hitting the target of four new accounts a month. I'd like to work with you on finding a way to get back on track. Will that work for your schedule?"

The key things to note about this positioning statement are:

- The concern is specific: "account openings."
- The focus is on the future, not on the past: "getting back on track."
- The meeting isn't to be a chewing out, but is previewed as a mutual problem-solving discussion: "I'd like to work with you on ways of getting back on track."

Step 2: The Discussion

During the discussion, you should:

1. *Put the employee at ease:*

    "Charlene, I know you are working on meeting your sales goal. I want to meet with you to make sure that all that work is going to get you where you need to go."

2. *Describe the performance issue:*

    "As you know, the goal is four account openings a month. You are running between two and three through the first quarter. Does that square with your count?"

3. *Get agreement on the problem:*

    "Would you agree that you need to find a way to improve on that record?"

4. *Ask future-oriented, neutral questions:*

    "Is it possible to reach the four-account goal?"

    "What might you try to get your closing rate closer to the goal?"

    "How can I help you?"

Avoid:
- Past-focused questions:

    "Why aren't you making the goal?"

- Accusatory questions:

    "You do care, don't you?"

- Closed questions:

    "Can you do this?"

---

5. *Listen to and encourage employee ideas:*

    "That's a good thought. What else might you try?"

Step 3: Agree on a Course of Action

After you and the employee have discussed a number of possible remedies, it is time to narrow the field and pick a course of action.

"Well, Charlene, I think you've got some pretty good ideas here. Let's narrow them down to the one or two best and decide how to go forward from here."

Step 4: Set a Follow-Up Date

At first blush, it may seem that most coaching situations don't need follow-up. Possibly, but we've seen enough situations where employees are reluctant to go back to a coach and straightaway admit, "That thing we talked about? It ain't workin'. No way."

A follow-up commitment on your part says that you want to know that the problem is solved. It also communicates to the employee that your concern isn't simply the whim of the day, to be forgotten tomorrow.

"Charlene, let's touch base in ten working days or so and see how your plan is working. Would the twenty-fourth or the twenty-fifth be better for you?"

Throughout this chapter we will be harking back to Dr. Tom's technique as the approach to addressing the Coach's Nasty Nine. We will not walk through every scenario to its conclusion, but instead will give you a very abbreviated version of how the discussion might flow. We will illustrate the positioning for each, and, where germane, some highlights for discussing the problem and reaching agreement on an action plan.

Simple Performance Adjustments

The coaching situations in this category are relatively easy to handle unless you avoid the issue, ignore the behavior, and hope "time" will change things. Delays will allow these situations to migrate from something you can address with an appropriate coaching intervention to a persistent performance problem that will mean big headaches for you and your team.

Getting the Rules Right: "What Do You Mean You Comp'ed Everyone's Meal?"

The standing rule in most organizations today is, "Do what it takes to make the customer happy." A great concept, but one that needs a lot of coaching to get right. Some employees, when told, "Do what it takes," interpret the mandate to mean that every day is two-for-one day. Others tighten the screws, fearing that a mistake made in good faith or an overgenerous gesture will send them to the unemployment line.

Situation 1: Charlie Gives Away the Store

Many restaurants today are embarking on "Satisfaction Guaranteed" customer service policies. The idea: If the customer isn't happy, give him or her something—dessert, an after-dinner drink, even a free meal, if necessary. Everyone gets it but Charlie.

A review of the week's receipts tells you that Charlie gave away three times as much stuff as anyone else. Your goal: To get Charlie's comps (complimentary giveaways) into line with the rest of the wait staff and the intent of your policy.

Begin by positioning the discussion:

You: "Charlie, I'd like to talk with you about the new Satisfaction Guaranteed program. I see that you've comped quite a few meals this week. The numbers seem a little high. Maybe there are some special circumstances that led to that, but it's also possible that I didn't do a very good job explaining it to you. When would be a good time to talk about the program and how it is working for you? Do you have ten minutes now?"

Discussion opener:

You: "Charlie, the purpose of the 100 percent Satisfaction Guarantee is to keep our customers coming back for more, and to give them tangible evidence that we can be counted on to deliver the food and service we promise. I'm very hopeful that the program will distinguish us in the market. And I'm glad you feel comfortable comping drinks and desserts and even meals.

"We have to be flexible in delivering on the Satisfaction Guarantee. I'm just a little concerned. As we discussed last week when we introduced the program, if we go all out—buy an entire group dinner—to resolve every small problem, we'll go broke—and we won't have any room left to wow customers if a larger problem ever occurs.

"Can you go over your approach with me so I can be sure we are operating the same way in our decision making?"

Although you *could* just tell Charlie to knock it off and stop giving away the store, you run the risk of his tightening up too much. The goal is to get Charlie to interpret the policy in a more appropriate (more controlled) way, not to stop him from comping food and beverages altogether. Accepting responsibility for not being *clear* in your initial explanation of how the policy should be implemented gives Charlie a face-saving out.

Situation 2: The Case of the Disputed Shipping Charges

Many businesses can and do waive incidental fees in order to strengthen their most profitable business relationships. At your travel agency, Mr. Bigbucks is never charged a fee for rush delivery. Absorbing the cost is a wise investment in keeping Mr. Bigbucks happy. When Charlene—a new agent—bills him, it's a coaching opportunity.

You:	"Charlene, Mr. Bigbucks just called me about the rush delivery charge you made to his account. Is now a good time to talk about it?"
Charlene:	"Sure. What's the problem?"
You:	"Charlene, you may not have been aware of it, but we don't charge Mr. Bigbucks for rush shipping."

Charlene: "That doesn't seem fair. I mean, we incurred the cost and we expect other clients to pay it. He's looking for permission to rip us off, $15 at a time."

You: "It might seem that way, but I'd like you to think about it as an investment. We're simply bending a policy to ensure that we keep a good client—a very profitable client. By eating the rush charge, we are actually protecting our revenues *more* than if we charged the expense back to Mr. Bigbucks.

"What can I do to help you feel comfortable knowing when to bill rush charges to our account instead of back to the client's?"

Coaching From Customer Reports: "And the Survey Says . . . ."

Most managers make a regular practice of posting customer comment cards, customer letters, and the results of surveys and mystery shopping. Fewer use these reports as an opportunity for individual coaching. But they are prime coaching opportunities, especially the ones that cite a specific incident and employee.

Situation 1: "That Charlene, She Walks on Water!"

These are a pleasure to deal with. *First,* share the comment card, letter, or phone call privately with Charlene. Thank her for her efforts, and ask what specifically she recalls about the incident. The more specific your praise, the more likely the performance will be repeated. *Second,* ask Charlene's permission to post the note, comment, or call for all to see. *Third,* if Charlene has done something quite out of the ordinary, ask Charlene's permission to share it with the team. *Caution:* Always err on the side of *privacy,* if there is a question in your mind.

Situation 2: "You Oughta Fire That Charlene Bozo!"

Now is when it gets nasty. If the letter or comment card is signed, your first step will be to follow up with the customer. You need more information before you can act in an intelligent way. If the complaint is anonymous, you need to think about three things:

1. Have you ever seen Charlene doing anything resembling the behavior described in the complaint?
2. Is there an opportunity here for you to gather your own information before talking to Charlene?
3. Is the "problem" that has been reported just too minor to warrant any sort of investigation?

Let's suppose that the offense is important and you can and do verify the details. You decide that it's an opportunity to do some coaching with Charlene. The dialogue might go something like this:

You:　　　　"Charlene, do you remember waiting on the Snodgrass party last night? They were at table 22."

Charlene:　"Sure, party of six. Looked like a business dinner. They ran up a good bill, but didn't tip well. Was there a problem?"

You:　　　　"Well, Mr. Snodgrass left me a note saying that his waitress was abrupt and rushed him through the wine selection."

Charlene:　"I remember that he really dawdled. Took him a while to choose—and the entrées were coming pretty fast last night."

You:　　　　"I called his office—the number was in the reservations book—and he's still a little hot. Not mad, but a little annoyed. I comped his bar bill and apologized.

"How would you feel about giving him a call, and talking with him a little bit yourself?"

Charlene:　"Well, I suppose I should. Yes, okay."

You:　　　　"Good. Here's his number. Now, let's rehearse what you're going to say to him. Maybe we can learn something about what he would have preferred you to do in that situation."

> *Situation 3: "That Charlene Stinks. I'm Never Coming Back to This Stupid Restaurant Again. Signed, An Ex-Customer"*

Now this *is* the pits. Someone is really upset, and you don't know who—or why—or what exactly to make of the comment.

Is the customer complaining about *service* or *body odor*? Or something altogether different?

The key here is to have a preestablished policy that states clearly your intention to follow up on all unhappy customer feedback, and to resolve any complaints as quickly as you can.

You: "Charlene, I received a comment card—unsigned— that sounds like you had an unhappy customer either last night or the night before."

At this point, Charlene can either recall the problem or not—or decide not to recall the problem. More than likely, she will recall it. If she doesn't, or claims not to, you are left with the "We want all our customers to enjoy our restaurant and to come back again. I know you wouldn't have purposely upset a customer" speech and an obligation to watch Charlene a little more closely than usual to see if something odd and possibly upsetting to customers has crept into her service repertoire.

Let's assume that Charlene remembers a Ms. Spitfire, who was upset and who might have left the nasty note.

You: "Let's assume you're right. What exactly went on that upset her?"

Charlene: "Well, I'm not sure, but she wasn't happy when I told her that the Wednesday Lasagna Special was all gone. I thought there were three or four portions left when I took her order."

You: "Do you remember how you broke the news to her?"

Charlene: "Well, I think I just said it. Like, 'Sorry, we're out of the lasagna. What else can I get you?' or something."

You: "Okay. How might you have done that differently?"

And from there, you are off into a normal coaching situation, working together to create alternative approaches.

Situation 4: You People Really Stink! I Waited Forty Minutes for a Table, and Then When I Got One, the Friday Fish Fry Special Was All Sold Out."

Generic, no-name complaints can also be an opportunity for coaching. Call the troops together for a three- to five-minute, preshift review of practices. Ask employees for ideas on making wait times work better. A caution: Don't go to the team on the basis of a single complaint. Use the complaint as a signal to gather more information. The "wait time and out of special" complaint *may* or *may not* have been an isolated event. Find out before asking the team for a fix. You risk drawing people's time and attention to a nonissue and leaving your team open to a performance failure somewhere else.

> *Situation 5: Coaching Around Hearsay—"Your Road Repair People Are a Bunch of Goof-Offs!"*

Municipal highway crews usually have little direct customer contact, although they are visible every time a citizen drives by a work site. What citizens see—or think they see—strongly influences their opinion of the highway department, and what they say about it to others.

A citizen calls you and reports that one of your employees was "sleeping on the job while my tax dollars are wasting away."

You: "Charlie, we had a call complaining that someone was sleeping on the job in Truck 88, your truck, this morning out on Highway 212. The caller said he saw feet sticking out the window. What's the scoop?"

Charlie: "That was me. Must have been when I was on my break."

You: "Charlie, we both know how important public perception is. What can you do to manage your breaks so that people don't perceive you as 'sleeping on the job'?"

Charlie: "Well, if I was working close, I could come in to base, like we do for lunch. But that doesn't make much sense when I'm way out on 212. I guess I just shouldn't get so relaxed when I'm in the public view."

The Slumping Employee: "I'm Not Concerned About Tom's Output Right Now. What I Am Concerned About Is Your Performance."

Sometimes a formerly stellar employee falls to earth. When a once bright and shining star now exhibits dull and tired performance, you may feel that, out of respect for past performance, you should overlook current performance—especially when Charlene is still a better producer than Tom or Joanne.

The issue has to be, "How is Charlene performing in relation to *her* potential?" If the answer is, "below par," it's your job to speak to her about the performance gap and discover what can be done to close it. Ignoring—essentially accepting—the performance slump does a disservice to Charlene, to the company, and to you as her coach.

Situation 1: The Sales Call Slide

Charlene has been one of your most consistent performers, so when the weekly sales reports show that Charlene is performing well below her norm, you address the issue in a coaching session.

You:	"Charlene, I noticed that over the past two weeks, you've averaged only 2.5 sales calls per day. You've been up around 3.8, 4.2, 3.9 calls per day. And so I'm concerned about the drop to 2.5, and I'd like to look at things to see what you can do to get back up to 4.0."
Charlene:	"I didn't want to tell you, but I guess you should know. I'm having troubles at home, and I'm just not able to concentrate. I'm in the middle of a divorce."
You:	"Well, a couple of things I'd like to say then, Charlene. One, I'm really sorry to hear that, and as you know, we do have an Employee Assistance Program. If you are feeling a lot of extra pressure right now because of this situation, I think they will be able to help you. So let me first suggest that you see them for help with that.
	"In the meantime, I want to focus on the job performance. Given all that you've got going on, how can you get *closer* to 4.0 calls per day?"
Charlene:	"Well, I have to make all these appointments about the divorce, and nobody wants to meet after five. I'm sorry, but that's the only time I can have those meet-

ings, and that's exactly the time when I should be
out on sales calls."

You: "Let me do this. You have a lot going on right now.
Think about how it's possible to reschedule some of
these appointments or calls, or in the short term
doing some flexible scheduling with your sales
calls—maybe going to a four-day workweek. And
then let's get back together at the end of the week
and figure how you can move back toward that 4.0
and what we can do to provide you with the flexi-
bility you need. And once we do, how you will keep
it in the 4.0 range."

Situation 2: The Never-Going-to-Make-It Employee

When a performance lapse is no longer temporary, one of
two things may be going on. It may be that the employee just
isn't right for the job and should be "made available to new
opportunities." But it may also be that you've inadvertently *created* a never-going-to-make-it employee.

When you hired Charlie as a hotel housekeeper, you knew
that he would not be the fastest, most efficient crew member.
However, his perfect attendance record with his previous em-
ployer and his genuine wish to do a good job made a strong
positive impression. You looked forward to adding a steady, de-
pendable member to your crew. After each shift, you meet with
Charlie to point out areas where he needs to improve: "You
missed vacuuming under the bed and wiping behind the sink in
several rooms." However, instead of improving, Charlie's performance is in a steady decline.

Change your coaching tactic. Instead of focusing only or
primarily on the poor marks, review the entire evaluation form
in item order. Thus, all performance—good and bad—will be
given equal attention.

You: "Charlie, I see your overall room score was 78. Last
time it was 76, so you are making progress to our goal
of 95. Bed making was a perfect 10. That's great—the
kind of performance that sets us apart. You lost points

on vacuuming. There was a can under the bed in one room, and dust bunnies in another. That's one thing you'll want to watch out for next time. The next item is bathroom appearance. . . ."

The result? If Charlie's performance can improve, it will improve. Chances are that at the end of another two weeks, you'll be proud to have Charlie on your team.

Performance Adjustments in Complex Times

What makes these next cases special is that in each, managers and supervisors—at least, some managers and supervisors—feel a special "Gee, do I have to?" reluctance to begin the coaching conversation. In several of them, the adage "This hurts me more than it hurts you" could actually be true *if* the coaching is delivered or received badly.

It is far better to coach in these situations than to do nothing. A reasonable employee will assume that, unless you tell him or her otherwise, he or she is meeting your expectations. When you take action only after months of inappropriate behavior, you shouldn't be surprised if the employee gets angry.

"Why is it wrong today if it was okay last week, last month, or last year?" asks employment attorney Jon Lewis, who has seen unaddressed performance problems blossom into lawsuits. "Bottom line," says Lewis, "the longer you wait to address a problem, the greater the chance an employee will sue, and win—or at least settle well."

The Employee Who Is Hard to Replace: "I Don't Want You to Get Mad and Quit, But . . . ."

The employee you hired because "anybody is better than nobody" will drive away customers, make you crazy, and alienate other employees. If you feel that you are being "held hostage," take a page from any SWAT team handbook: Never give in. Confront the situation positively with a simple four-part strategy:

1. *Write your fear down* on a piece of paper or describe it to yourself.
2. *Assess, is this really likely to happen?* Then ask yourself, "Can I afford to take this risk?" and "Can I afford not to?"
3. *Plan the encounter to minimize the risks.* Write out the exact words you will use to tell the employee how you expect him or her to behave in the future.
4. *Hold the coaching session.* Hold it soon—don't hide behind a month of planning as a clever way to avoid the uncomfortable.

Situation 1: Low Unemployment

As manager of a fast-food restaurant in a city with a 2 percent unemployment rate, you know that your employees can find other jobs, paying as well if not better, with little or no effort. Still, when you notice Charlie chewing gum on the job and failing to articulate clearly when speaking into the microphone at the drive-thru window, you realize that you must correct those behaviors.

> *Name your fear.* The fear is simple: If Charlie doesn't like being coached, he will leave, and you'll be short-staffed for weeks.
> *Assess the situation.* Charlie might get mad and leave, but he seems to like his work team—and even to like you. So, you decide Charlie is not likely to quit over this. You decide the risk is worth it.
> *Plan the encounter.* You plan the encounter, using Dr. Tom's Sure-Fire Coaching Conversation model.
> *Hold the session.* You address the issue with Charlie at his next shift.

One additional note about the low-unemployment hostage situation: If you aren't paying a competitive wage, no amount of coaching will help. Having said that, dollar compensation is only one of the reasons people stay at a job. You have to pay *well* above the standard for your area to hold your employees hostage to a job they hate. Coaching can and does demonstrate positive care and appreciation.

Situation 2: Low Employee Commitment

You know that for many of your team, this job is their second job. You overhear Charlene telling a coworker, "Look, to be perfectly honest, the only reason I'm here is that my mom says I have to work or I can't keep the car." You've observed that Charlene is slow to serve customers, that she doesn't follow through with cleanup, and that she arrives late and leaves early. Your coaching challenge: Motivating Charlene to do the job correctly and completely. It is up to you to help Charlene find another reason, more motivating than "Mommy made me," for doing a good job.

You: "Charlene, you don't look like you're having fun on the job. I saw you smile maybe once in the past two hours. I know that being here at work isn't your first

	choice, but since you have to have a job, let's figure out a way to make the experience as good as it possibly can be. What do you like best about working here?"
Charlene:	"The people. I get to work with my friends. They're great. But some of the customers are really, really bad."
You:	"I'm glad you like the people here. It's obvious they like you as well. But I'm concerned that some of the customers are a problem for you. Could you give me an example?"
Charlene:	"Well, there's like this one guy who comes in every day, and like he watches me cut the bagels and if it's one little bit off center, he tells me that I'm doing it wrong."

Now, you are off to the races talking with Charlene about ways she might deal with those situations that make her less than keen about her job.

You:	"Charlene, do you think that if we have a couple more of these chats about ways to think about and work with some of these problem customers, that would help you feel better about the job?"
Charlene:	"Well, it might. I just don't know what to do with some of these people."
You:	"I understand completely. On my first job, the toughest thing for me was learning about customers. It just takes practice."
Charlene:	"Well, okay."
You:	"Good. I appreciate your cooperation. Why don't I check with you tomorrow and see how you're doing? Would that be all right?"
Charlene:	"Okay!"

Situation 3: Scarcity of Skilled Labor

As manager of a professional plumbing business, you feel very lucky when you are finally able to find and hire another licensed plumber. Your business is thriving—in large part, you believe, because at least one member of your team is on call twenty-four hours a day, your crews show up promptly, and they leave the customer's house looking better than when they arrived.

When a repeat customer calls you at home, you learn that your newest hire, Charlene, wasn't responding to pages during her turn to be on call. You realize that the risk of losing Charlene is outweighed by the risk of losing customers and your need to be fair to the other members of the team, so you plan to coach Charlene as soon as possible.

You: "Charlene, I'm concerned because no one could reach you on Saturday when it was your turn to be on call. I'd like to talk with you about it."

Charlene: "To be honest, I'm really not too keen on the Saturday thing. I don't want to work weekends. I know you need my help; I'd like to just work during the regular workweek."

You: "Charlene, I understand your feelings, and that is a decision you have to make. I need people with technical plumbing skills, and I need people with customer contact skills, and I need people with commitment. All three of those make a professional plumber. Our edge in the market is our twenty-four-hour commitment. That means that taking turns covering on weekend days and after hours is part of the job.

"Saturday is behind us now—whether it was your mistake or my mistake for not being clear doesn't matter. But it can't happen again.

"What I'd like you to do is to take the rest of the day off with pay to think about whether or not you're willing to make that commitment."

Your success will depend on convincing Charlene to actively choose to live up to your performance expectations or to "voluntarily separate" from the company.

Situation 4: Managing Diversity

Especially sensitive in these politically correct times are situations in which managing diversity seems to add a layer of complexity to coaching a lapsing employee. If coaching issues and outright performance issues are not being addressed promptly and appropriately with all employees, your formal coaching efforts in this situation may indeed look unusual in the day-to-day landscape. Apply a high standard of customer contact consistently to all employees, and you won't be guilty of treating employees differently on the basis of race, gender, sexual preference, physical ability, or any other non–work-performance-related standard. If your coaching system is in good shape, proceed in this coaching session as you would in any other coaching session.

Focus on job-related performance. It's the best way to ensure that you are applying standards consistently and providing the level of coaching and feedback that employees need from you. This doesn't mean treating everyone absolutely, positively identically—it means treating people as individuals, but applying standards consistently. Even in sensitive situations, the steps of Dr. Tom's Sure-Fire Coaching Conference still apply.

There are times when the service professional's job is made more difficult by customer, or even coworker, prejudice. It's difficult to be nice to, much less work closely with, someone who dislikes you. When Charlene accuses a customer of prejudice, and uses this as an excuse for not working with her, you have a special coaching challenge.

You: "Charlene, I'm concerned because Mrs. Glok told me that you weren't giving her the level of service attention that she expects. It's her perception that you don't want to work with her. What's the situation?"

Charlene: "Oh, Mrs. Glok. She doesn't like me because, to quote her, I'm 'one of those people.' She's the one with the problem. She can't stand to work with me."

Continue the discussion with questions like:

You: "Tell me more about your experience with her.

                "What has she said directly to you?"

At this point, you may want to refer to your organization's guidelines or training programs for dealing with customers who are insulting or intimidating.
Future-oriented neutral questions, such as

"How might you implement some of the strategies from the training class?"

or

"How can I help you?"

will move you and Charlene to agreeing on a course of action. It will be important to follow up with Charlene to ensure that the situation with Mrs. Glok is improving.

Situation 5: With Friends Like These . . .

Anticipating your promotion from service representative to manager, you fear that your buddies in the ranks may pressure you to give them special treatment, or to make exceptions to the rules based on your friendship. Assessing the situation, you decide that the best defense is a good offense. You plan to hold one-on-one conversations with each of your best work buddies. The meat of your message:

You: "Charlie, as the manager there are going to be times when the organization will require me to make decisions that may be unpopular. I want you to know that I will always be straightforward with you and that I will always listen to whatever you have to say."

Later, when Charlie asks you for a special favor, you have a firm foundation for saying no:

Charlie: "I know it's short notice, but I want to take tomorrow afternoon off. Can you make an exception to the one-week-notice policy?"

You: "Is this some sort of emergency?"

Charlie: "No. I just, you know, have a lot to do at home."

You: "I'm sorry, Charlie. I know how things can pile up, but I need you here. I told you there would be times when I have to make unpopular decisions, and this is one of them. I have to live with the policy on this one."

The Employee You Don't Own, and Can't Fire: "You're Not the Boss Over Me."

You need to be sensitive to the turf boundaries in your own organization. Certainly, it would be stepping out of line for you to personally confront the persistent performance problems of an employee who doesn't report to you—that is the purview of that employee's manager or supervisor. However, when a quick coaching session will prevent the off-the-mark behavior from becoming a real performance problem, or the situation from being blown out of proportion, you should address it.

Situation 1: Dr. Bad Mouth

You manage a group of nurses for an outpatient clinic. Doctors are considered very important customers. They send the patients to the clinic for same-day surgery. Dr. Smith uses the clinic every week. But Dr. Smith isn't the most pleasant guy on the block. This "Chicago Hope" wannabe swore at a nurse last week, and when she complained, he told her it was her job to "take it." After surgery, the nurse found you and said that she *didn't* have to take it. She even threatened to quit. Your coaching challenge: Dr. Smith's abusive manner and belligerent bad mouth.

You: "Doctor, I need to talk with you about something that occurred in surgery yesterday."

Dr. Smith: "What might that have been?"

You: "I wasn't there, but Charlene was very upset—she

	said that you swore at her, and when she spoke to you about it, you weren't very receptive."
Dr. Smith:	"A surgical team is supposed to run like a Swiss watch, and if it doesn't, I let them know it in no uncertain terms."
You:	"We all believe in that, Doctor. And if there is a performance problem, I want to know about it, and so does the team. We need your input to keep us sharp.

"Charlene was upset about the language you used to call out the problem. Your voice was angry, and your words were demeaning."

Dr. Smith:	"Look, if she's so sensitive, maybe she doesn't belong in the O.R."
You:	"Doctor, our goal is to have a climate of mutual respect in the operating theater. I know our team has great respect for your skills. If I'm going to keep a strong team in place, I need your help."
Dr. Smith:	"Okay, sure. What do you need from me?"

From this point, you are in a problem-solving and action-planning mode with Dr. Smith.

Situation 2: The Officious Office Service

You have an office services contract with the same firm that manages your office space. You asked Charlene, the staff word processor, to enter corrections in an important client report. She promises to complete it by 2:00 P.M. At 3:00, she gives it to you. Not only is it late, but it is riddled with typographical errors.

Because of the contract situation, your coaching challenge begins with a conversation with her staff supervisor.

You:	"Charlie, do you have a minute? I have some concerns about the document Charlene just did for me. I'd like to talk with her about it to make sure we are on track for future assignments, but I thought I should touch base with you first."

Charlie: "Thank you. Is it a situation where you need me to give Charlene some correction?"

You: "Well, I would be happy to talk with her directly—or, if you prefer, the three of us could sit down together."

Charlie: "If you're comfortable talking directly with Charlene, that's great. Please let me know if you have an ongoing problem or if your concerns aren't resolved."

Now you are ready to meet with Charlene. You will have a normal coaching conversation.

Troublesome Personal Habits: "What Do You Mean, I Stink?"

No one likes to confront another human being over a personal habit or hygiene issue. Note, please, the number of times Miss Manners and Dear Abby and Ann Landers are asked for how-to advice on this very topic.

As a manager, you have no choice; if a customer, colleague, or peer of the offender complains, you need to grab a clothespin and your coach's hat and go at it.

Situation 1: Chatty Cathy

Cathy is a hard-working Information Systems Support representative who prides herself on good relationships with her callers. She's also a long-winded talker. When two customers comment, "She's very nice, but I don't have time for all the chit-chat," it's time for the manager to take action.

You: "Cathy, I know that you know that our customers expect friendly, courteous, *and* efficient service. And you know our users appreciate your friendliness. But I'm a little concerned because two customers have commented that they feel you spend too much time on the phone chatting with their employees."

Cathy: "What do they want? Are you saying that I should let them sit in silence while I work on the problem?"

You: "Of course not. The concern here is about balancing the friendly talking and the efficient problem solving. What might contribute to the managers' thinking that their employees are on the phone just shooting the breeze instead of problem solving?"

Cathy: "Well, sometimes a user and I will get talking about something while I'm waiting for the software test to run, and that might look like we're not working to someone else."

You: "And if that 'someone else' is their boss, the customer who pays for our support . . ."

Cathy: "Oh, I see the problem."

From here, you are into a regular problem-solving discussion.

Situation 2: Hugging Hank

Today's business environment is particularly touchy about touchy-feely behavior. Hank loves to give hugs, and many customers comment about how much they look forward to their hug from Hank. However, when one customer complains that the hugging makes her uncomfortable, the manager has to address it.

You: "Hank, I need to talk with you. We both know that one of the things that sets our business apart is our friendly service. A lot of our customers have been our neighbors for years. Others are new to our area—still getting settled in and becoming comfortable. I received a comment from a customer who said she felt uncomfortable being hugged."

Hank: "I just try to treat everyone friendly. People love my hugs!"

You: "I know it—I've had positive comments about it. I think, Hank, this is an issue of comfort zones. Our established customers, those who've grown up with us, who have been in this community a long time, who maybe even attend your church, they know you and

	love to hug you back. Some other customers may not be comfortable in that same situation."
Hank:	"I guess I see what you mean. I just want them to know that I care about them, 'cause I really do."
You:	"I know you do, Hank. How can you keep that level of caring while making sure that every customer feels comfortable here?"
Hank:	"I'm certainly *not* going to stop hugging my friends."
You:	"And I wouldn't want you to. How can we make sure the new friends we're making in the community feel comfortable?"
Hank:	"Well, I guess if it's someone I don't see and hug regularly outside of work, I won't hug them when I'm at work."
You:	"That sounds great!"

Situation 3: Smelly Sam

Few things are more personal than bad breath or body odor. Many managers prefer to duck this one: "I wrapped up a Speed-stick and put it in his pocket with a note," confided one. Another admitted to sending an anonymous E-mail message. We prefer to be more straightforward. Employees have a right to expect supervisors to give them correction—even uncomfortable correction—to their face.

You:	"Sam, this is an uncomfortable conversation for me, and I expect it will be for you, too. You and I both know that we have to create a welcoming environment for our customers. Customers have complained that your body odor makes them uncomfortable. So that's why I need to talk with you."
Sam:	"What are you saying? Are you saying that I'm dirty? That I don't wash?"
You:	"Sam, what I am saying is that customers have complained about your body odor. I don't know the reason for the odor. I do know that other people's perceptions of body odor, cologne, cigarette smoke, or whatever are often different from our own percep-

tions. What's important at work is that we are aware
of, and sensitive to, how customers perceive us.''

Sam: "They're just hypersensitive. You don't think I stink,
do you?''

You: "What's important here is that it has made customers
uncomfortable. Are there any special circumstances I
need to know about, or is there anything I can do to
assist you? For example, if you need an extra uniform,
we can get that for you. What do you think?''

Situation 4: Farting Freda

No, we did not make this up. While certain bodily functions
are inevitable and sometimes uncontrollable, there are employees who take pleasure in creating bodily noises for the purpose
of embarrassing coworkers. In second grade this was funny,
maybe. In the work environment, it may need to be addressed
by the coach.

You: "Freda, you and I both know that the way we manage
our work environment will affect the quality of our
work. We want a work environment that is comfortable and pleasant, that is respectful and supportive.''

Freda: "Of course. I always do my best.''

You: "I'm glad to hear it. Freda, this is an uncomfortable
conversation for me, and I expect it will be for you,
too, because I need to talk with you about a workplace
behavior that is making your coworkers uncomfortable—your continual passing of gas.''

Freda: "What? What do you mean? *Who* complained?''

You: "Your continual passing of gas is disruptive and very
uncomfortable for your coworkers. It is negatively af-
fecting our work environment. Are there any special
circumstances I need to know about or for which we
need to make some accommodations?''

Freda: "No. What's the big deal? Everybody laughed.''

You: "Well, it's disruptive. I really appreciate your commitment to continue as a positive player on our work
team. How can we move forward from this?''

Freda:	"Well, if that's the way everyone feels about it, I'll stop trying to add humor to the day."
You:	"Freda, we all like to have some humor in our work-day, and I'm not trying to discourage all humor. I know that there are lots of ways for you to add humor and brighten the day."

This coaching session will be most successful if it is followed up with a few problem-solving sessions in which you ensure that Freda understands that it's still good to engage in appropriate humor that enhances the environment for everyone.

Situation 5: Temperamental Ted

Sometimes the coaching challenge doesn't involve personal habits, it involves fragile personalities.

Several of the employees at your music store are musicians who seem to have stereotypically artistic temperaments. Today, a music teacher called, upset that Ted told her student that the violin the teacher recommended was "poorly made" and "not worth the money." You need to coach Ted on the importance of deferring to the opinions and choices made by music teachers— key influencers in the buying decision.

You:	"Ted, I got a call from Mrs. Anderson at the Middle School. She was upset because she sent one of her students here to buy a specific violin. Mrs. Anderson said that you pushed the parents very hard to buy a much more expensive violin. What gives?"
Ted:	"Yes, I remember. The teacher recommended a very substandard instrument. If you are going to play the violin, seriously play, you should buy the best. So that's what I told them."
You:	"Ted, I understand your thinking. And I know that you're a great judge of violin quality. I know that for you, quality is the first consideration. What do you think were the parents' considerations in choosing a violin?"
Ted:	"Well, I would think that they would want quality."

You:	"Okay, quality would be important. But what other considerations might they have in buying a violin for their son?"
Ted:	"Well, I suppose they might worry that he wouldn't take proper care of it or that he might lose it or break it. And, a lot of students don't keep up with their music."
You:	"I think you're right. In addition, this family has some economic limitations, so Mrs. Anderson was trying to steer them toward a violin that they could afford."
Ted:	"I didn't consider that aspect of it."
You:	"It's important for you—for all of us—to make suggestions and offer information, but in the end we must show deference to the customer's choice. In this case, we really have two customers in this transaction: the student and his parents, and the music teacher."
Ted:	"Next time, I won't be so quick to second-guess the music teacher's recommendation."

Trouble on the Team

Some performance issues are less involved with employee-to-customer encounters, and more with employee-to-employee, or even department-to-department, interactions. While these are often out of the direct sight of the customer, they do affect the level of service the customer receives, and should be addressed as barriers to Knock Your Socks Off Service delivery.

Reluctance to Change: "I Know You Hate the New Computer System."

Like customers, employees aren't always keen on change. Just ask any manager who's witnessed the introduction of a new computer system, the merger of departments or, worst of all, the dreaded re-cube-ification. It's okay for employees to have opinions about changes, and to express them. In change situations, it's important that you don't rise to the bait and step in too soon. People need to vent—and mourn.

Situation 1: System Changes

Last month, your company made a major computer system change. The new system links sales, support, manufacturing, and logistics. It does more overall, and less for each particular department. Your customer support employees miss some of the idiosyncrasies of the old system. You overhear Charlie talking to a customer:

Charlie: "I'd like to help you, but our new computer system won't let me do that. You know how it is—you get something working just how you like it, and then they change it on you."

You discover that others are making similar comments, and you decide to hold a short team meeting to address the problem. During the meeting you:

1. State that you are in sympathy with the difficulty of learning a new system.

2. Ask for input on the shortcomings of the new system and problems with it that they have noticed so far.
3. After you've listened to their complaints and concerns, ask the employees to log their problems with the system for two weeks. This will give you—and the team—an opportunity to gauge the real impact of the problems.
4. Promise to go to the systems group with the problems and ask them to work with the department on solutions or work-arounds.
5. Hold a discussion about the potential negative impact of complaining to customers about the computer system.
6. Brainstorm things to say to customers in those instances where the new system prohibits them from serving customers immediately or in the same manner as in the past.

Situation 2: What Happened to Charlene?

You and Charlene have decided that she might be better suited to another occupation, one not involving customer contact. That, of course, brings up questions from both customers and coworkers. You understand that there is a need for discretion here, and that there can be a legal problem if you say too much to other employees about the conditions under which an employee has left. You also know that while you don't want to say more than necessary, you will have to give your team some direction on how to think and talk about Charlene's departure.

Charlie: "So, I see that you finally fired Charlene. What took you so long?"

You: "I'm sure you understand the circumstances and reasons for Charlene's leaving are between Charlene and me. So it's really not something that you and I can discuss."

The key is to answer only the question you were asked. Answering a question you weren't asked, or that was implied, will get you into trouble. If you're in doubt of what to say or do, ask a question in return:

Charlie: "What's the deal, now that she's gone?"
You: "Why do you ask?"
Charlie: "Well, a lot of people are going to be surprised that she's gone. In fact, I saw her just this morning in the employee parking lot."
You: "Charlie, the best thing for us to do is to keep in mind two things. One is that Charlene is no longer here. The other is that some of her customers may be asking where she is. If a customer asks where Charlene went, you may say that she left to pursue other interests. If the customer wants her address, offer to forward a note. I'll see that Charlene gets it."

Intramural Moaning: "I Don't Care if You Don't Like the Marketing Department or Jane. You Still Need to Work With Them."

It's an old story. Marketing hates manufacturing, and Jane can't stand Kathy. It would be great to just wave a wand and chant the magic words, "We are all members of a team. We value each other. We are as one." But life doesn't work that way.

Situation 1: "Deal With It"

Two days after you take over as manager, Charlie asks to schedule a meeting. Topic? What a pain Charlene is. Later that day, Charlene corners you to say the same thing about Charlie. There is no documented performance issue with either employee individually, so you decide to confront them on their mutual dislike. You call them both into a meeting in the conference room.

You: "I've asked for this meeting because each of you has independently let me know that you are having difficulty working together. I want you to understand that you do need to work effectively together. I'd like to see you work this out on your own, but I am happy to help you. How would you like to proceed?"

Charlene and Charlie may agree to fix up their differences without you, or they may ask you for a form of third-party mediation. Either way, you will need to follow up to ensure that things are working, or to take appropriate next steps.

If Charlene and Charlie refuse to work it out, or if Charlie is part of an entire faction of employees who all hate Charlene, the situation will be much nastier to resolve. And it may no longer be a coaching opportunity. If Charlene and Charlie *won't* work together, give them the "opportunity" to work apart. Yes, even firing may be appropriate. It's not about blaming one side or the other. It's about putting an end to behavior that is destructive to Charlene, to Charlie, to the work team, to you, and to your customers.

Situation 2: When Accounting Says No

Product delivery to a key customer was delayed three weeks. Charlene asks you if she can refund the shipping fees as a gesture of atonement. You approve. So you are surprised when Charlene comes to you and announces, "Accounting says no." It seems that when Charlene took the refund request documents over to the accounting department, Charlie told her he didn't think the customer should get a refund—after all, lots of things are delivered late and "All you folks in customer service do is give away money."

You have two coaching challenges. First, affirm to Charlene that she did the right thing.

You: "Charlene, you did the right thing, and I'm going to back you up on this one."

Second, and more challenging, you need to coach Charlie in accounting.

You: "Charlie, I need to talk with you. I understand from Charlene that you told her that you wouldn't process the refund."
Charlie: "Well, it doesn't seem necessary. I need to watch the bottom line."

You: "Charlie, you and I are both in the same boat. And I appreciate your diligence. But this is a $5,000,000 account."

Charlie: "We have a lot of large accounts at Acme. We can't go giving shipping costs away at these margins."

You: "I understand that. But we're three weeks overdue on this one, and they aren't happy. I think this is a worthwhile investment. So, I'd like you to look at the refund in the larger perspective of what's right for the company, what's right in terms of our long-term strategic goals."

If Charlie still refuses:

You: "I understand what you're saying, but I'm going to have to take it up to another level."

When You Aren't the Expert: "Hey, I'm the Computer Expert, So You Just Do Your Manager Stuff and Leave Me Alone to Do My Job."

When you aren't an expert, it's seldom a good idea to try to bluff those who are—especially when you are the manager. Offer incorrect information, and you'll find yourself backpedaling and losing face—and you'll find your team second-guessing any other information, help, or advice you have to offer.

When you know or expect employees to challenge your personal expertise, be clear in your own mind about what you don't know. And be confident about what you do know. Sounds simple, doesn't it? Actually, it is.

Situation 1: "Look, You Have to Be a Techno-Nerd to Really Understand This"

Charlie is a technical wiz and proud of it. He always knows the best way to find out why the software is misperforming and to get it back up to speed. His interpersonal skills are not so sharply honed. When you overhear Charlie lose patience with a customer, you see a coaching opportunity. Your challenge: Help Charlie improve his customer interaction.

You: "Charlie, I know that I can only hear one side of the phone conversation, but I'm concerned, and I would like to take some time to talk with you about your last call. Do you have time now?"

Charlie: "Sure."

You: "Tell me about the call—who it was, what they needed."

Charlie: "It was Ms. Doe from Acme. What a dummy. I kept telling her what to do, but it took forever to make her understand. I could go into the details of the problem, but I don't think it would make sense to you."

You: "Charlie, my concern isn't about the technical side of Ms. Doe's problem. I know you are probably the best problem solver on the team. My concern is about the interpersonal side. From what I heard, you sounded pretty frustrated."

Charlie: "I was."

You: "We need to look at the call from Ms. Doe's perspective. Think about calling someone you don't know about a problem you don't really understand. What do you think her internal reaction to the experience might have been?"

Charlie: "Well, she sounded confused to me. I suppose she might have been intimidated."

You: "Yes, Charlie. That's my best guess, too. It's very clear that you know how to fix Ms. Doe's problem. I'd like to work with you on ways to work with someone like Ms. Doe without getting so frustrated. We have to anticipate and manage how a Ms. Doe hears, sees, feels, or experiences the conversation. I'm still learning our software myself, so I think I'll be able to help you with Ms. Doe's perspective."

> *Situation 2: "Look, You're New Around Here. You Don't Understand the Way We Do Things and Why We Do Them That Way."*

You were just hired to manage the telephone sales support department for an industrial manufacturing firm. You've managed phone sales before—in the packaged food industry. Your *new* company makes replacement parts for earthmoving equipment.

You schedule an introductory group meeting with your sales support team. You know that you will need to use this opportunity to:

1. Acknowledge what you don't know.
2. Demonstrate your respect for the team's expertise.
3. Answer questions about your approach to management.
4. Solicit input on the team's toughest customer problems *and* the decisions they will need you to make, *and* the situations you will be expected to arbitrate for them with customers and other departments.

Here's a possible opener for the meeting:

You: "I'm delighted to be part of this team. Everything everyone's told me about this company and about this department, everything I've seen in terms of our customer satisfaction surveys, tells me that you know your job and you do it well.

             "Some of you may not know about me. I come from over five years of working with the telephone sales support area for a packaged food company. I've spent many years full-time on the phones—I actually started in college, taking inbound calls for a retail catalog company.

             "I've never worked in industrial manufacturing. That's both good and bad. The bad part is that I don't yet know the specifics of our products.

             "But there's also an upside. I come from a different place, I have a different set of experiences. So, my belief is that we can combine my past successes and experience with yours to make us better than we already are. So I may come to you and say, 'What if we did it this way instead of that way?' My hope is that you will feel very comfortable saying back to me, 'You are out of your mind, and here's why.' And we can talk that through, and out of that discussion may come a better way of doing things that we are already doing well right now.

"My charge, from my boss, is to find a way to start taking market share back from Acme. I think that, together, we can do just that."

``Management (and coaching) is doing those things necessary to deny people who work for you the unpleasant opportunity of failing.''

—Management Maxim

10

"Can We Talk?" Peer Coaching

''Camp counselors have been using the
buddy system for years.
It's about time that we did the same.''

—A Manager

Once upon a time not very long ago, the average supervisor had responsibility for five to fifteen people. In today's downsized, reengineered organizational environment, that figure is closer to thirty. The result, as one frustrated customer service manager expresses it, is: "I don't do management—I do crowd control."

At the same time, many organizations are experimenting with "self-directed" work teams, assemblages of peers who manage themselves and their assigned work, without day-to-day direct supervision or even coaching—unless they reach out for it.

These two facts of modern organizational life mean that employees in many organizations see a lot less of their managers, and managers have significantly fewer coaching/helping opportunities than was the case just five or six years ago. Yet the need for coaching is as great as or greater than ever before. The solution of choice: peer coaching. In this arrangement, employees of the same level, without the traditional leverage of a reporting or boss/subordinate relationship, are being asked to observe, provide feedback, and coach one another on substandard and problematic performance. But peer coaching concerns more than

correction. Peer coaching also involves peers helping one another to succeed by providing upfront help and sharing valuable, hard-won tips and tricks.

On the positive side, well-trained peers, schooled in the techniques of coaching and the nuances of effective interpersonal communication, can be an asset. If you've ever had a colleague pull you aside to warn you that "The boss is on a tear; don't bring up the Johnson account" or simply to let you know that something was unzipped or unbuttoned or stuck between your teeth and marring your sunny smile, you know how valuable peer feedback and information sharing can be. On the other hand, the negatives of peer coaching are easy to imagine. If you have ever been approached by someone you didn't respect who offered to "give you a little advice," you have a grasp of the potential problems.

Peer coaching—some people prefer to call it peer "support"—succeeds when the conditions are right and the ground rules clear. Specifically, a successful peer coaching venture requires:

- A supportive culture/environment
- Awareness of the limits—and strengths—of peer coaching
- Training in the skills of giving and receiving feedback
- Practice in the art of accepting peer coaching

The Supportive Environment

If your organization has a history of interdepartmental warfare—marketing and operations speak only through their U.N. ambassadors, supervisors say "well done" only when they are ordering steak, and frontline customer relations are more adversarial than collaborative—then peer coaching will probably fail in your organization in about 2 1/2 minutes.

On the other hand, if your organization is tolerant of mistakes—if it treats most mistakes as opportunities for learning and not punishment—and if employee/management and customer/company relations are trust-based and generally affable, then peer coaching has a very good chance for success.

Awareness of the Limits

Though peer coaching is in vogue, it is not a be-all-and-end-all opportunity. Rather, it is a way of leveraging your skill as a coach by investing some of that skill in others. It is a supplement to, rather than a substitute for, the coaching you provide. And it most definitely is not a way to get out from under the responsibility of dealing directly with employees who have chronic performance problems or for delegating your role in passing out "well done's" and positive reinforcement.

There are five fundamental axioms we think are essential to creating a stable foundation for effective peer support:

1. *Peer coaching is not backseat driving.* Ever try to drive cross-country with a passenger who has mastered the art of the "lecture question"? You know the type: "Is the recommended nighttime speed along this stretch above 65?" or "I'll bet it's really

hard to tell how closely you're following someone along here at night, isn't it?" Peer coaching is about giving direct, clear feedback and advice, and doing that only when permission has been sought and given, or when the feedback is solicited. Peer coaching is about asking questions, sharing information, and mutual learning about work.

2. *Peer coaching is not group therapy.* Leave the tea leaves and horoscope reading at the door. Supporting peers in their efforts to do well is not a parlor game. No one in the workplace has a right to probe anyone else's psyche or motivations. The peer coaching process, just like supervisory coaching, is about "The facts, Ma'am. Just the facts." And a limited set of facts at that— observable, amendable workplace behavior. There is a trend today to shower teams, especially self-managed teams, with psychological and personality tests under the banner of creating group harmony. Approach these well-meaning interventions with care and caution. The goal of every management technique is to improve productivity and, through that, business results. Helping others live brighter, fuller, happier lives is great in its place—but that place is *not* the workplace.

3. *Helping out is the spirit of peer coaching.* Peer coaching is not permission to blow off steam, express anger, or otherwise give a colleague "a piece of your mind." The onus is on the giver to answer three questions before opening his or her mouth to offer Charlie a little help:

- Is Charlie really having trouble with a customer, colleague, or situation? (Or are you just uncomfortable with Charlie's particular operating style?)
- Is the problem clearly Charlie's, as opposed to a problem Charlie is involved in, but not one he owns or is obliged to resolve?
- If you don't offer to intercede, will the situation you perceive or the behavior you observe cause an irreparable problem for the organization—or for Charlie?

If the answers to all three questions are yes, then you have an opportunity to offer assistance or advice.

4. *Peer coaching, like supervisor coaching, provides balanced feedback and support.* We have mentioned several times that coaching is a positive act, not a negative one—that a coach owes an employee laudatory as well as corrective feedback. This is even more true of peer coaching. Where self-directed teams are at work and peer coaching is used to supplement supervisory coaching, it is critical that multiple positive peer feedback systems be in place.

5. *Peer coaches respect the "rule of once" and the "right of refusal."* It is an even bet that the last time someone offered to "give you a little feedback," the tone of voice and attitude made the words sound like "give you a piece of my mind," and you felt trapped. Peer coaching is a two-way, voluntary event. The cornerstone is respect for others' wishes.

The "rule of once" goes like this: You get to give your feedback and advice on an incident, a situation, or the way a peer approached a problem or a task once. And only once. The assumption has to be that Charlie heard and understood you. Beyond that, he is free to accept your input, disregard it, or hold it in abeyance. Unless Charlie asks you to "Go over that thing about dealing with Delwood down in Dallas again," you are under only one obligation: Leave it alone once you've said your piece.

The "right of refusal" is a corollary to the rule of once. You and we and Charlie have a perfect right to say "thank you" and ignore peer input. We even have the right to not listen to peer input—as in "I know you get along better with Delwood than I do, but I'm working it out my way. Thanks for offering." And as the rule of once prescribes, *that* is *that*.

The Four-Step Peer Coaching Model

There are four parts to the peer coaching model. They fit together to frame a one-on-one discussion that is both offered and welcomed in a spirit of mutual benefit, that is focused on behaviors rather than personalities, and that is focused on future improvement rather than on defense of past performance.

Step 1: Positioning

To ensure success, the peer support encounter must be conducted in a positive environment. Positioning does two things. First, it allows the coaching peer to *state why the session is needed.*

The peer coaching session should focus on specific actions and behaviors, and may be prompted by something the coaching employee directly observed, something he or she overheard, or something reported by a customer:

- "I noticed that you were having some difficulty processing the return for that last customer."
- "I couldn't help overhearing the end of that last phone call. You sounded a little tense."
- "Mr. Smythe told me that you yelled at him."

Hearsay comments from other employees or even from a boss are generally *not* an appropriate focus for a peer support session. If the peer support environment is to remain strong, the coworker or boss in question should make his or her concerns known directly.

The second part of positioning is to *ask permission to discuss the performance.* Asking permission is about communicating that the peer would like to offer assistance, and that he or she will back off if assistance is unwanted. State the reason for the session *before* asking permission so that the peer knows what is to be discussed before giving a go-ahead or a please back off.

How does a peer ask permission to act as a coach? The exact wording can vary, but here are two acceptable examples to work from:

- "Charlie, if you have a minute, I can show you some techniques that have worked well for me."
- "Can we talk about it? I may be able to give you a different perspective."

So an entire positioning statement would sound like this:

- "I noticed that you were having a little bit of difficulty processing the return for that last customer, Charlie. If

you have a minute, I can show you some techniques that
have worked well for me."

- "Mr. Smythe told me that you yelled at him. Do you want
  to talk about it? I may be able to help. I've dealt with him
  a lot."

If you are thinking to yourself, "That sounds a little stilted;
I don't know if I can talk to a colleague that way," you are right
on. The language *is* a little stiff. In practice, peers experienced
with coaching one another use pretty informal language:

Charlene:	"That sounded rough. What's up?"
Charlie:	"Mrs. Glockenspiel again. She really gets under my skin."
Charlene:	"Yeah, she gets to me, too. I've been getting along with her pretty well lately, though. Wanna talk about it?"

The more experience peers have with one another, the better
able they are to give and receive nonverbal and subtle cues that
say whether the receiver is open to the feedback, or "not just
now."

Step 2: Discussion

The discussion is an opportunity for the person being coached
to clarify the situation, as the volunteer coach listens and asks
questions. It is important that the person offering the support
acknowledge the positive things the peer did and affirm the
peer's good intentions in the witnessed, overheard, or reported-
on customer transaction.

Charlene:	"Charlie, you seemed to have your hands full with Mrs. Glockenspiel. What was going on?"
Charlie:	"She swore I'd overcharged her last week, but she was all wet about what she'd bought. It was more than she remembered."
Charlene:	"She was determined to make you admit you were wrong?"

Charlie: "Something like that."
Charlene: "You seemed to have her close to under control, given the circumstances. What were you saying to her?"
Charlie: "Well, I kept apologizing while I looked for her last transaction."

Step 3: Advice Giving

After the two discuss what actually happened, Charlene can now offer appropriate feedback and advice. The focus here is not on berating a colleague for past performance or asking him or her to define past behavior, but on ensuring future success. Advice giving must be forward-looking, specific, actionable, and, above all, respectful.

Step 4: Closure

The peer support session should end on a positive note. A "thank you for letting me offer support"—not necessarily in those words—should be implicit in the close. If the peer coach hasn't learned anything personally helpful from the encounter, it's likely that the session was more lecture than discussion, and possibly berating rather than supporting. If appropriate, closure may include an offer for further assistance.

Charlene: "Charlie, thank you for letting me talk with you. To tell you the truth, it's comforting to know that I don't get all of the Mrs. Glockenspiel calls! How can I help out the next time you get one?"

The Art of Accepting Peer Coaching

If giving feedback and coaching to a peer is dicey, receiving it is doubly so, especially the first time or two that you are the recipient. Most of our experience with feedback and advice from others is negative—and emotional. Rick Maurer, author of the *Feedback Toolkit* (Productivity Press, 1994), says that accepting feedback from others is difficult because of an "unwanted guest" at the table that he calls SARA—an acronym that stands for:

Surprise or Shock: "This can't be true, can it? I mean, this can't be me he or she is talking about."

Anger: "Who said that?" "How dare you!" "Who are you to be talking to me like that?"

Rationalization: "Oh, sure, but do you really know what it's like out there on the line? Have you ever dealt with that old bat?"

Acceptance: "Okay, I hear you. Yeah, I see what you mean. I can try that."

Given the universality of this reaction to uncomfortable information, it is important that:

1. You don't go into a peer coaching arrangement without the knowledge and understanding of everyone to be involved.
2. Everyone understands the rules of conduct—and agrees to them.
3. You do some training, some skill practice in a controlled environment.

Some tips for being a good recipient of unpleasant news:

1. *Allow yourself to say no* to the offer if you aren't in a frame of mind to hear what your peer has previewed.

2. *If you choose to listen, listen.* Don't argue, interrupt, make faces, or stamp your feet. Listen. Listen to the words and the message. Be analytical: Is the peer telling you something about *content* (what you know or don't), about *style* (the way you did something), or about a *situation* you are involved in?

Defensiveness—arguing, rebutting, or reinterpreting what the peer is saying to you—simply stops the input.

3. *You can and should ask for clarification or more information,* if you don't understand something you've been told. But do so gently and without a tone of accusation or anger.

4. When you think you understand the feedback, or when you think peer coaches have helped you all they can, *thank them for their efforts.*

5. *It is okay to take a "time-out"* or otherwise call a halt to the proceedings if Maurer's friend SARA comes creeping into the conversation. Coaching—or being coached—when either party is upset or angry is unprofitable *and* unwise.

Note: We've been focusing here on the worst case: Accepting unpleasant and negative information, and a peer's advice on how to mend or change a problem situation. Most peer coaching situations do not involve emotionally charged, highly negative information. Most peer coaching involves small, helpful "I didn't know that—thanks!" sorts of situations.

The Peer Support Model in Action

A peer support session may be prompted by something a peer observed, overheard, or was told by a customer.

Situation 1: The Contentious Encounter

The retail store environment is fraught with challenges for even the most seasoned customer service professional. Kasha was restocking when she noticed Charlene in a discussion with a customer. "No, you're wrong," Charlene insisted. "We never carried anything from that designer." Correct or not, Kasha knows that rule one in this store is, "Look for ways to make the customer right." Here's how she offered support to Charlene:

Positioning:
Kasha: "Charlene, I was stocking while you were talking to that customer, and I saw that you were having a disagreement. Is it something I could help with?"

Discussion:
Charlene: "I hope you can. She was asking about some Sylvia

brand stockings, and we never carried those. She claimed she'd bought them here, and wondered why didn't we have any more. She just wouldn't believe me that we've never carried Sylvia brand."

Kasha: "Did you ask her if another brand might work for her?"

Charlene: "I didn't really get a chance. She was just so irritating."

Advice giving:

Kasha: "I get frustrated too when customers act like they know more or better than I do. It's hard to say 'You're wrong' without saying 'You're wrong.' They get defensive and stop listening. The last time I had one of those I said, 'I'm sorry. I don't remember seeing that brand. I can tell our manager that you've requested it. In the meantime, might another brand work for you?' I think it went pretty well. She settled for a sheer leg, anyway."

Closure:

Charlene: "I can try that. If I pick up the product, she'll have something to look at. That could change the subject. Thanks."

Kasha: "That's a good idea, too. Glad to help."

Situation 2: The Venomous Voice

Charlie: "What a stupid call! This customer didn't have a clue!"

Tim: "We talked about clueless customers in the training class last month. They had some good tips. Do you want to hear some of them? We could do it over lunch."

Charlie: "Yeah, that would be great."

Discussion (over lunch):

Tim: "So, what happened?"

Charlie: "She wants to have her nose fixed and thinks that her policy should pay for it. I explained that only medically necessary surgery was covered and asked if she was having any health problems because of her nose. Well, the conversation didn't go well, and she ended up yelling that low self-esteem was a health problem and did we want to pay thousands of dollars for years of therapy, or just a few hundred dollars for a nose job? I was ready to give her a nose job!"

Tim: "I've had a few like that myself. Clueless. It makes me mad and frustrated. I've been working on not letting that distract me from the real problem: helping the member understand and accept the limits of her policy. The instructor pointed out that customers will argue with us about policy limits, but when a manager says the exact same thing, the customer will say 'Okay.' Before you let yourself get mad, you might consider transferring the caller to Sandra."

Closure:
Charlie: "I'll try that next time. Thanks."
Tim: "This was a good review for me, too."

Situation 3: "You Tell That Clerk She's the Rudest Person I Ever Met!"

Charlene was generally considered one of the friendliest people working in the clinic. She handled the difficult job of patient scheduling with a calm that Amhad, a nurse's aide, had often envied. So, he was taken aback when a patient commented to him, "My blood pressure may be way up. I had to change my next week's appointment, and that clerk was just the rudest girl!"

Positioning:
Amhad: "Charlene, earlier today a patient said something to me that I can't really believe. You know Mrs. Myrtle Carter? She told me that when she rescheduled her

next appointment, you were rude to her. Can we talk about it?''

Discussion:

Charlene: "The dreaded Mrs. Carter. Normally I can handle her, but today, on top of everything else, well, she was just too much. I guess I didn't do a very good job of hiding that."

Amhad: "Maybe it would help just to talk it through. I'd be happy to listen."

Charlene: "Amhad, it's just that everyone expects me to smile, and be nice, and talk to four people at once, and get interrupted by a nurse asking for a chart, and, well, when it's like that, a Mrs. Carter can just push me over the edge."

Amhad: "Sounds like you anticipated a tough encounter when you saw her coming."

Charlene: "It's predictable. She always needs to change this or move that. . . .''

Advice giving:

Amhad: "It seems like you usually have Mrs. Carter under control and that today was just an exception. When I have those days, sometimes I just have to put everything on hold and step outside for a couple of minutes to regain my composure. I know that when I'm busy, I forget how busy you are, but I know the nurses could cover for you for a few minutes—just like we do during scheduled breaks.

"Since Mrs. Carter will be back here soon, you may want to consider giving her an extra-friendly smile when she comes in and an 'I'm sorry things were so hectic when you were here before.' I think you are one of the most even-tempered people on the staff."

Closure:

Charlene: "Thanks for listening. I'll try that."

Training for Positive Peer Coaching

Effectively offering and responding to peer support is a skill. Some employees will be immediately comfortable with it; others will not. We strongly recommend that you teach employees a process like our four-step peer coaching model, and give them ample opportunity to practice offering and receiving peer coaching in a safe environment. If your organization has a professional training function, it makes sense to avail yourself and your team of this resource. Your organization may even have developed or purchased a peer coaching training course (see Chapter 11, ''Recommended Resources''). There is little, if any, benefit in reinventing the wheel. Set up a meeting with your training coordinator and schedule away.

If a formal training program isn't available to you, ask yourself, ''When do I have or will I have an opportunity to teach this skill to my team?'' Some managers choose to do it as part of several regularly scheduled staff meetings. Other supervisors have scheduled special training sessions. Still others have taken advantage of formal annual training events. Identify the time and the place that will work for your group and commit to it.

After you have committed to doing the training, plan the learning. Here is an outline for a typical ninety-minute session.

- Welcome the group; thank them for coming.

- State the objective: ''We need to recognize the importance of providing feedback to each other, and to become better providers and receivers of positive peer support.''

- Introduce axioms. Discuss each, what it means, and why it's important.

- Introduce the model. Ask participants to describe a positive peer support discussion. What would happen in it? How would it begin? How would it progress? What would be the best outcome? Then compare that discussion to the four-part model. The best model is the one you and your team are most comfortable with. Our four-part model can serve as a template, but add your own variations if you need to.

• Brainstorm situations. Create a list of situations in which a peer might offer support to another peer. What might the peer observe? Overhear? Be told by a customer?

• Create role-plays. Work in teams of two or three. Each team should pick one situation and write a role-play that demonstrates each part of the peer support model.

• Perform the role-plays. Perform as many role-plays as time allows. After each, discuss how the coaching peer might feel and how the "coachee" might feel. Point out how this type of peer support benefits both employees and the entire organization.

• Summarize the key points. Thank the group for participating.

As with any skill or behavior you've asked your staff to demonstrate, you will have to take time to observe and coach your staff as they do peer coaching.

Variation: When the Peer Involved in Peer Support Is You

Unless you are the only manager or supervisor in your organization, you will have plenty of opportunities to model giving and receiving peer support. If you can't do both, and do them well, your direct reports probably won't have the patience to learn and hone the skills either.

Consider Charlie, a store manager for a fast-food chain. Jim, the area financial manager and Charlie's peer, was visiting at Charlie's location. While he was there, Charlie corrected an employee for improper food handling. Jim was concerned about the way it was handled, so he waited for the situation (lunch rush) to clear and then addressed it with Charlie.

Positioning:
Jim: "Charlie, I was a little taken aback by your interchange with Sandy. Can we talk about it?"

Charlie: "Really? Well, if you think I was doing something wrong . . ."

Discussion:

Jim: "I know you were concerned with correcting Sandy's performance, but while that was going on, I noticed the customers at the counter and they looked very uncomfortable—even intimidated."

Charlie: "I didn't even think about them. I saw Sandy handling food without a plastic glove and instinctively jumped in. I've told her about this before."

Jim: "She hasn't been responding to your coaching, and you're getting a little frustrated?"

Charlie: "You bet I am!"

Advice giving:

Jim: "You know I agree that we can't compromise on the food-handling standard. But we also have to keep in mind the effect on the customer. How can you handle it next time so that you don't draw the customers' attention to the situation or make them feel uncomfortable?"

Charlie: "I just need to stop and think first. Next time, I'll make sure to deliver my feedback out of sight of the customers."

Closure:

Jim: "Thank you for letting me mention that to you. I know it's easy to forget that customers can see everything. But it's important to keep corrections backstage, so to speak."

> ``People want a more collaborative workplace. That requires trust. Trusting relationships need time and stability to develop.''
>
> —Geoff Bellman

11

Recommended Resources

As we mentioned in the introduction, enhancing your customer service knowledge is a never-ending process. With that in mind, we offer the following short listing of books, newsletters, games, training videos, and seminars with an emphasis on coaching skills.

Books

Anderson, Kristin. *Great Customer Service on the Telephone*. New York: AMACOM Books, 1992.

Anderson, Kristin, and Ron Zemke. *Delivering Knock Your Socks Off Service*. New York: AMACOM Books, 1991.

Anderson, Kristin, and Ron Zemke. *Knock Your Socks Off Answers: Solving Customer Nightmares and Soothing Nightmare Customers*. New York: AMACOM Books, 1995.

Bell, Chip R. *Customers as Partners: Building Relationships That Last*. San Francisco: Berrett Koehler, 1994.

Bell, Chip R. *Managers as Mentors: Building Partnerships for Learning*. San Francisco: Berrett Koehler, 1996.

Bell, Chip R., and Ron Zemke. *Managing Knock Your Socks Off Service*. New York: AMACOM Books, 1992.

Berry, Leonard L. *On Great Service: A Framework for Action*. New York: Free Press, 1995.

Charney, Cy. *The Manager's Tool Kit: Practical Tips for Tackling 100 On-the-Job Problems*. New York: AMACOM Books, 1995.

Connellan, Thomas K. *How to Improve Human Performance: Behaviorism in Business and Industry*. New York: Harper & Row, 1978.

Connellan, Thomas K. *How to Grow People into Self Starters*. Ann Arbor, Mich.: The Achievement Institute, 1988.

Connellan, Thomas K., and Ron Zemke. *Sustaining Knock Your Socks Off Service*. New York: AMACOM Books, 1993.

Deeprose, Donna. *The Team Coach: Vital New Skills for Supervisors and Managers in a Team Environment*. New York: AMACOM Books, 1995.

DePree, Max. *Leadership Jazz*. New York: Dell Publishing, 1992.

Fournies, Ferdinand F. *Coaching for Improved Work Performance*. Blue Ridge Summit, Pa.: Liberty House, 1978.

Fournies, Ferdinand F. *Why Employees Don't Do What They're Supposed to Do—and What to Do About It*. Blue Ridge Summit, Pa.: Liberty House, 1988.

Hargrove, Robert. *Masterful Coaching*. San Diego: Pfeiffer & Co., 1995.

Kinlaw, Dennis C. *Coaching for Commitment*. San Diego: Pfeiffer & Co., 1993.

Leeds, Dorothy. *Smart Questions*. New York: McGraw-Hill, 1987.

Maurer, Rick. *Feedback Toolkit: 16 Steps for Better Communication in the Workplace*. Portland, Oreg.: Productivity Press, 1994.

Miller, James B. *The Corporate Coach*. New York: Harper Business, 1993.

Mink, Oscar G., Keith Owen, and Barbara P. Mink. *Developing High Performance People: The Art of Coaching*. New York: Addison-Wesley, 1993.

Shula, Don, and Ken Blanchard. *Everyone's a Coach*. Grand Rapids, Mich.: Zondervan and Harper Business Publishers, 1995.

Stowell, Steven J., and Matt M. Starcevich. *The Coach: Creating Partnerships for a Competitive Edge*. Salt Lake City: Publishers Press, 1987.

Weiss, Donald. *Fair Square and Legal: Safe Hiring, Managing and Firing Practices to Keep Your Company Out of Court*, 2d ed. New York: AMACOM Books, 1995.

Zemke, Ron. *The Service Edge: 101 Companies That Profit from Customer Care*. New York: New American Library, 1989.

Zemke, Ron. *Service Recovery: Fixing Broken Customers*. Portland, Oreg.: Productivity Press, 1995.

Newsletters

Customers First, Dartnell Publications, 4660 N. Ravenwood Avenue, Chicago, IL 60640.

On Achieving Excellence, TPG Communications, 555 Hamilton Avenue, Palo Alto, CA 94301.

Supervisory Management Newsletter, American Management Association, New York, NY 10019.

Training Directors' Forum Newsletter, Lakewood Publications, 50 S. 9th Street, Minneapolis, MN 55402.

Other Resources

Building Customer Partnerships. Video presentation with Chip R. Bell. Audio Video Campus, San Diego, Calif.

Coaching for Top Performance. Video. American Management Association, Watertown, Mass.

Creating Star Performers. 6-audiocassette program with Thomas Connellan. Nightingale Conant, Chicago, Ill.

Customers From Hell and the Ten Deadly Sins of Customer Care Board Game. Performance Research Associates, Inc., Minneapolis, Minn.

The Helping Hand. 2-video series. Video Arts, Chicago, Ill.

Knock Your Sox Off Service. 4-video series starring Lily Tomlin. Mentor Media, Pasadena, Calif.

Leading the Service Professional. Customized training program offered by Kaset Inc., Tampa, Fla.

Managing Extraordinary Service. Customized training program offered by Kaset Inc., Tampa, Fla.

On the Phone . . . With Kristin Anderson. 6-video series. Mentor Media, Pasadena, Calif.

Oops! Time for Service Recovery. Video staring Ron Zemke and Chip Bell. Salenger Films and Video, Santa Monica, Calif.

About the Authors

Ron Zemke is a management consultant and researcher, who has become one of the best-known and most widely quoted authorities on the continuing service revolution. As senior editor of *Training* magazine and a syndicated columnist, he has covered the emergence and development of the global service economy. Ron has authored or co-authored twenty-three books including the five-book *Knock Your Socks Off Service* series. In 1994, he was awarded the Mobius award by the Society of Consumer Affairs Professionals, and in 1995 he was named one of the "New Quality Gurus" by *Quality Digest* magazine.

Kristin Anderson is an internationally recognized customer-service workshop leader and keynote speaker. She also has extensive experience in focus-group and survey research. Her writing has appeared in numerous publications including *HR Magazine*, *Boardroom Reports*, *Training* magazine, and *Mobius*. Kristin has co-authored three of the five volumes of the *Knock Your Socks Off Service* series, and acts as host on six films on the customer-service process. She is also author of *Great Customer Service on the Telephone* (AMACOM).

Performance Research Associates is one of North America's premier customer-service / customer-relations / service-quality consulting firms. PRA has offices in Minneapolis, Dallas, and Ann Arbor, providing training and consulting services to clients in North America, Europe, South America, and the Pacific Rim. The *Knock Your Socks Off Service* series draws on the experience and work of the partners of Performance Research Associates,

Inc. Readers interested in information about presentations, consulting, or other PRA services may contact the firm's Minneapolis office at 1-800-359-2576.